CARTRIDGE BRANDS

OF

THE BRITISH ISLES

Ken J. Rutterford

Published 2016 by arima publishing

www.arimapublishing.com

ISBN 978 1 84549 688 3

© Ken J Rutterford 2016

All rights reserved

This book is copyright. Subject to statutory exception and to provisions of relevant collective licensing agreements, no part of this publication may be reproduced, stored in a retrieval system, or transmitted in any form or by any means, without the prior written permission of the author.

Printed and bound in the United Kingdom

This book is sold subject to the conditions that it shall not, by way of trade or otherwise, be lent, re-sold, hired out, or otherwise circulated without the publisher's prior consent in any form of binding or cover other than that which it is published and without a similar condition including this condition being imposed on the subsequent purchaser.

arima publishing
ASK House, Northgate Avenue
Bury St Edmunds, Suffolk IP32 6BB
t: (+44) 01284 700321
www.arimapublishing.com

ACKNOWLEDGEMENTS

The information and the photographs that go to make up this book are due to the kindness of so many people that go back over a very long period in time. This could well be as long as fifty years. These folk range from shop keepers, shop assistants, librarians and collectors of cartridges. Many of these people may now not be with us having moved on to pastures new. The majority of the cartridge photographs shown here have been taken due to the kindness of their owners. They were taken at very many places over those many years that have gone by. Because of this and the long periods in time, I am not able to roll off a list of names. My memory is not now what it once was, to do so would cause me to leave a lot of people out. To those of you who consider that you have given me help over the past, I here thank you.

Having just said what I have, there are a few people that I feel I must mention by name. First my old friend Ronnie Crowe who did so much when helping me in getting my first book published called, 'Collecting Shotgun Cartridges'. It is this book which I have put together as an updated replacement to that book.

Many cartridges in my own collection never got photographed. Through the kindness of Terry Strong I was able to photograph a few of these. Several times he brought trays from his collection down stairs so that I could take photographs and he kindly helped with the lighting, thank you Terry.

A lot of fresh to me information was sent or given to me from people who go, or are associated with metal detecting. I here extend my thanks to Angie and Dave Stone and also Neville Cullingford from South Hampshire. I also thank Colin Silk from West Berkshire. From these people I have had, and still do get fresh Information on old cartridge firms as they literally continue to dig up the past.

,

A Selection of Shotgun Cartridges.

CONTENTS

ACKNOWLEDGEMENTS   3

A Selection of Shotgun Cartridges   4

INTRODUCTION   6

THE FOLLOWING DRAWINGS   7

USING THIS BOOK   8

THE ABREVIATIONS   10

SECTION ONE
The written listings   11 – 84

Unidentified Cartridges   85

SECTION TWO
The Illustrations with written listings   86 –232

A few of the Unidentified   234 – 235

SECTION THREE
Additional drawings to those in my
Book, "STAMPINS on SHOTSHELLS"
    236 -245

INTRODUCTION

Now that I am in my mid-eighties and registered disabled due to arthritis, I became in need of finding some activity with which to keep my mind occupied. At some cartridge club meetings I had noticed that several members still carried with them the very first book that I had published called, 'Collecting Shotgun Cartridges'. Once that book had been published I became very unhappy with the result. So much so, that I strive to do better. With thanks to arima publishing, they have since published three books for me on old shotgun cartridges. These are, 'Cartridge Drawings Now and Then', 'Stampings on Shotshells' and 'Cartridges of The British Isles'. Although I felt happy with these three books, I now realise that not one of them became a replacement for my first book. They were not suited for carrying to meetings or arms sales etc. Having now gleaned more information, this book is intended to be an up-dated replacement for my first book that has long since gone out of print.

This book is half the size of my other three books. It only contains shotgun cartridges that were either all brass or had paper tubes and were closed with an over shot card retaining the shot load using a rolled turn-over. It only covers the firms and their cartridges of the British Isles and this includes the whole of Ireland. What it does not do is list cartridge brands that were closed by six or eight fold crimps, unless the brands had been closed by both means.

Several people have said to me that if the book contained coloured illustrations then they would buy it. The problem with showing too many coloured illustrations is that it would make this book too large and clumsy. Because of this the listings of the firms and their cartridge brands are now in two sections. Section One is the listing without cartridge illustrations. Section Two is with these coloured illustrations. Following on from Section Two is Section Three. This last section covers the many head-stamp drawings which I have made since my book 'Stampings on Shotshells' was published and these drawings I considered are relevant to the cartridges of the British Isles.

Slightly reduced, the front cover of Baily's Magazine, No 167. Now 140 yreas old. See inside of the rear cover.

THE FOLLOWING DRAWINGS

All of these following drawings have been made since the publication of my book, 'Stampings on Shotshells'. You may find several that are similar to those that are shown in that book, but they will differ due to the size of the percussion cap or the letterings. Most of the head-stampings that are being shown here were used at some time or another by the firms of the British Isles. All the same, I may have included a few foreign stampings. Many of these firms from time to time imported into these isles foreign cases. I have decided to show some of these that I think were most likely used. Let's face it, some of these have only come to my notice because they were found in this country by people when they were metal detecting.

As has always been my practice, I have given each drawing an individual number. In order to help you in understanding my numbering sequence, I will now give you a run down on how each of these numbers was placed together. You will find that the first letter to each number is 'H'. This indicates that it is a head-stamping drawing. Following on from this is either the letters 'F' or 'S'. The letter 'F' stands for 'First Hand'. The letter 'S' stands for 'Second Hand'. When I have had a cartridge head, a photograph or a foil rubbing to work from, Then I have given the drawing the letter 'F'. In other cases I have only had a rough sketch made by some other person that I could work from. In these drawings the percussion cap or the letterings could be of the wrong size, but the lay-out should be correct. It is these drawings that I have given them the letter 'S'. The third letter will either be a 'C' or a 'P'. I have used other third letters, but I will not worry you here with them as they are not among the following drawings. These two letters just give the type of percussion. The letter 'C' standing for 'Centre fire' and the letter 'P' standing for 'Pinfire'. Following on from these first three letters shown is the actual number that is given to the drawing. On a very few drawing you will see that after the drawing number there may be '/R'. This on ending to a number usually indicates that it is a very early stamping. This '/R' refers to it being a raised stamping. The details of the stamping that is shown are stamped in the opposite direction as to the cartridges that are being manufactured today.

Since my book, 'Stampings on Shotshells', I have made many other head-stamp drawings other than what I have included in this book. As these are either modern or are not current to this book, they are not shown here. It is obvious that there must be very many other stampings that I have never had the chance to draw. I guess that I will now not live long enough to draw all of them.

The rear cover of Baily's Magazine for January 1874.
Note the addresses given for KYNOCH & COMPANY.

USING THIS BOOK

All the way through this book I have endeavoured to keep its size down to a minimum. In order to do this I have had to keep the printing small and make use of some abbreviations. The list of these abbreviations will be found on the page following this insertion. Once you have familiarized these abbreviations, all of the understanding will become clear.

I had intended using far more of the coloured illustrations, but the size of this book dictated to me otherwise. For this reason the firms and their cartridge brands have to be inserted in two sections. If you are looking for a particular firm and you are unable to locate it in Section One, then you must try Section Two. I have only been able to list in this book the information that has come my way. You may quite well know of some other that is not in this book. Well that is what is called sod's law. I know for a fact that there is far more than what I have listed. Much more will continually be found by old advertisement, cartridges, cartridge remains that will be unearthed by metal detecting. I have just had to cry knife at this present time in order to produce this book.

About twenty years ago, my late wife and I made the move from the country into the town. It was not a move that I wanted to make, but like so many other working country people, it became one of those things. At that time I then decided to sell my large collection of old shotgun cartridges. This was a decision made at the time which I have later grown to regret. Wrong decisions can be made at a time, but once made there is no going back. Should you be a person that has purchased some of my books then you will know that I have made many hundreds of drawings of shotgun cartridges. In order to have done this, over the years at club meetings and other collectors premises, I have taken hundreds of photographs in order to get sufficient data to be able to make those drawings. It is from these old photographs that I have used, for many of the coloured illustrations. Many of those photographs were taken in poor light and in not the best of conditions. They were taken with various cameras and at those times I was more interested in obtaining enough data to make drawings than what I was in trying to obtain first class photography. At the time when I owned my own collection, then I did not need to take photos of cartridges that it contained. Due to various reasons such as, cameras, developing, lighting conditions and printing, many of the colours are not true to life. For an instance, some of the orange have taken on a reddish hue. I only wish that I could have done better, but these illustrations should give you an inclination as to what they once looked like.

Due to space and also my lack of knowledge, it has not been possible to give all of the gauge or bore sizes that those brands were marketed in. One must also realise that many of the brand names were sold over a lengthy period in time and had been loaded into various cases, both British and imported.

Where I have written the words,' Shown Above', this refers to the illustrated cartridge and not any of the drawings that may be shown to its sides. Any such drawings shown are just making use of the space and giving extra interest. All of

the drawings were at some time used on cartridges by that firm but not necessarily on the illustrated cartridge. These drawings are of motifs, over-shot cards or head-stampings.

For some of these old firms, they go back in time to the start of breech loading, In the case of some, I do not have much information to go on. It might be just as little as what has been seen on a rare old cartridge head that some kind person has passed on to me having found it while metal detecting. This was a hobby that I once enjoyed myself while out in the country and along with my wife. Due to age and my health it is one of the many things that I cannot do any more. With most of the coloured listings I have just shown one cartridge by that firm. Where a firm may have been a little larger than most, or had marketed more brands than most, then I have been forced to give it more space. In this case, more than one coloured illustration may be shown. Also possibly more of the small drawings that accompany those coloured illustration. Here and there I have shown a coloured drawing when a photograph was not available. Also a provisional drawing that I have made from old cartridge remains just for the record.

As I have previously stated, I have done my best to include all of the information that I have at the time and to minimise the size of this book for easy handling. As this book with its listings is all alphabetical, to save space, I have decided not to include an index.

THE ABBREVIATIONS

Ad......Address or more than one address.
Am.....Ammunition manufacturer (As described by the firm).
Cl.......Cartridge loaded (A firm that stated that they loaded).
Cr.......Circa (Period in time).
Cx.......Cartridge expert (What a firm called its-self).
Ds.......Depatment stores.
Es.......Estate cartridge (Cartridge printed for a private estate).
Ga......Gun and ammunition dealer.
Gd......Gun dealer (May also deal in other items).
Gg......Gauge or bore of a gun.
Gm.....Gun maker (As called by the firm. May have sold tackle).
Gs.......Gun smith.
Gt.......Guns and tackle (As a firm called its selling trade).
Id.......Implement dealer (Agricultural).
Im......Ironmonger (Retail or wholesale or both).
Kb......Known Brands (Name given to the cartridges).
Lm......Leggings maker.
Mg......Motor garage or motor dealers.
Nk......Name not known. (Or not always listed in the research).
Nt.......Note.
Pc.......Private cartridge (Loaded to order by a private person).
Rd......Road.
Rm.....Remarks (History details etc).
Sm......Saddle and horse harness maker.
Ss.......Shooting School (Shooting tuition).
St.......Saint or Street (Saint as in St Andrew).
Un......Un-named cartridge.
Wm....Wide market (Country wide etc).

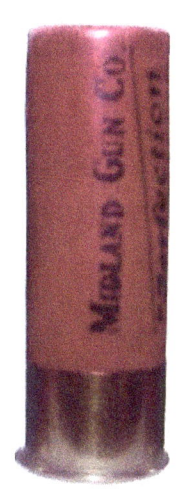   

SECTION ONE
The Written Listings

ACCLES ARMS, AMMUNITION & MANUFACTURING CO. [Am].
Ad; Perry Bar, Birmingham, Warw (W. Midlands).
Kb; Un.
Rm; This firm was founded when Grenfell & Accles ceased. They were known active Cr, 1896-1899. Their name has been seen on stampings only

HENRY R. ADAMS. [Im]. Ad; 120 High St, Cediton, Devon.
Kb; Yeo Vale.

J. H. ADAMS & SONS. [Im]. Ad; Littleport, Cambs.
Kb; Eley Gas-tight Cartridge Case.

ADAMS & CO.   Ad; Finsbury, Islington, London N4.
Kb; Nk.
Rm; Their name has been seen on a stamping on cartridge remains.

R. J. ADGEY.   Ad; 99 Peter's Hill, Belfast, Northern Ireland.
Kb; De Luxe, De Luxe Special, Favourite, Universal Metal Lined.

ADGEY & MURPHY.   Ad; Belfast, Northern Ireland.
Kb; Nk.
Rm; Their name has been seen on a stamping on cartridge remains.

EDWARD ADKINS. [Gm or Gs]. Ad; 194 High St, Lewes, Sussex.
Kb; Nk.
Rm; Was known active in 1882. Cartridge remains have been found.

T. ADSETT & SON. [Gm]. Ad; 101 High St. Later at, 90 High St, Guildford, Surrey.
Kb; Smokeless Cartridge.

AGNEW & SON. [Gm]. Ad; 79 South St, Exeter, Devon.
Kb; The Devonia, Ejector, Exon Smokeless, ISCA, Special Smokeless.

AGRICULTURAL EXECUTIVE COMMITTEE (A.E.C.).
Rm; See, H. M. GOVERNMENT OF GREAT BRITAIN, in this cartridge list.

ATKIN GRANT & LANG. [Gm}. Ad; 7 Bury St, St James's, London SW1.
Kb; The Raleigh.
Rm; Other brands that had been seen were crimp closed.

JOHN ATKINS (DUNMANWAY) LTD.   Ad; Dunmanway, County Cork,
Republic of Ireland.
Kb; Supreme Brand Cartridges.

ATKINSON. [Gd]. Ad; 31 Oxford St, Swansea, Glamorgan.
Kb; The Grand Fiale.

T. ATKINSON. Later became, T. ATKINSON & SONS.
Ad; 19A Strickland Gate, Kendal, Westmorland (Cumbria).
Kb; The Ajax, The Kendal Castle, The Kent, The Kentdal, The Reliable.

K. ATTRILL.   Ad; Pyle St, Newport, Isle of Wight.
Kb; Nk.
Rm; Information that came my way was that cartridges were once loaded on their premises.

AUTOMATIC SHRAPNELL CO. [Manufacturer]. Ad; 36 George St, Edinburgh, Lothian.
Rm; They manufactured John's Patent Shrapnell Shells. They were made in several sizes and were sold to other firms for loading into cartridges in place of the normal shot load. They gave better grouping over a longer range.

E. BAILDHAM & SON. [Im]. Ad; Stratford upon Avon, Warw.
Kb; The Duck Fowler, The Extra, The Standard.

CHARLES STUART BAILEY. [Inventor and possibly a cartridge manufacturer].
Ad; 8 Barmards Inn, Holborn, Middlesex (Great London). Also at, Waltham Abbey, Essex.
Kb; Un (F. Joyce case).
Rm; In 1882 he patented a gas-check for a central fire cartridge. This had an extra thin layer of brass that covered the primer cap. F. Joyce & Co Ltd, used this patent.

C. T. BAKER LTD. [Cl and Im]. Ad; Market Place & Norwich Rd, Holt. Also at, Sheringham, Norfolk.
Kb; Nk.
Rm; There was no know family connections between them and Joseph Baker & Son of Fakenham. I have never seen a cartridge by them. All of their remaining unloaded stock was handed in to the police and destroyed.

FREDERICK T. BAKER. [Gm and rifle]. Ad; 29 Glasshouse St, Piccadilly Circus. Later at, 64 Haymarket St, London SW.
Kb; Baker's Bakerite, Baker's Best, Ejector, Fred T. Baker's Vermin Smokeless.
Rm; Fred was known active in Glasshouse St, Cr 1905, and in Haymarket St, Cr 1913.

J. C. BAKER. [Im]. Ad; 48 Foregate St, Worcester, Worcs (H & W).
Kb; Baker's Special Bull's Eye Cartridge (Eley-Kynoch ICI case).

SYDNEY W. BAKER. [General merchant]. Ad; Crowcombe Station, Somerset.
Kb; S. W. Baker's Deadsure Special Smokeless Cartridge.

JAMES BALDWIN & SONS.   Ad; Morville St, Birmingham, Warw (W. Midlands). Also in, Glasgow and London (Ad's Nk).
Kb; Nk.
Rm; An 1896 advertisment illustrated ther own name on a printed over-shot card.

BALLS.   Ad; Bungay, Suffolk.
Kb; Nk.
Rm; Shot gun cartridges were once loaded on their premises.

BALLS BROS. [Im]. Ad; 64 Queen St, Newton Abbot, Devon.
Kb; Smokeless Cartridge.

J. J. BALMFORTH. [Engineers and Im]. Ad; Aughton St, Ormskirk, Lancs.
Kb; Balmforth's ORM Smokeless, Balmforth's Special.

HENRY BAMFORD & SONS. [Id, Im]. Ad; Market Place, Uttoxeter, Staffs.
Kb; Mow-em-down, The Plough.

JAS GAY BANFIELD & SONS LTD. [Im]. Ad; Tenbury Wells, Worcs (H & W).
Kb; Unitro Cartridge Case.

THOMAS WILLIAM BARNETT. [Im]. Ad; Sturminster Newton, Dorset.
Kb; The Crown.

H. BARNWELL & SONS LTD. [Cl, Mg and cycle manufacturer].
Ad; Hartley Wintney, Hants.
Kb; The Hartley Special Smokeless.

BARRATT & SON. [Gm]. Ad; 48-49 High St, Burton-upon-Trent, Staffs.
Kb; Un (Name on over-shot card only).

BARTON SMITH.
Rm; Filed under SMITH in this cartridge list.

A. BATES. [Gm]. Ad; 22 Sun St, Canterbury.
Also at, Sturry & Whitstable, Kent.
Kb; The Challenge, The Imperial Cartridge, The Rabbit.
Rm; A. Bates was known active , Cr 1910.

A. T. BATES. [Gm]. Ad; 3 St George's Gate, Canterbury.
Also at, Whitstable, Kent.
The Canterbury, The Challenge, Ejector.
Rm; I also had the Ad, 3 St George's St. This could be the same Ad. There is obviously a connection between this and the previous entry.

E. BATES.   Ad; Eastbourne, Sussex.
Kb; Nk.
Rm; This name and town found on a stamping on cartridge remains.

E. R. BATES & SONS.   Ad; 71 Burgate St, Canterbury, Kent.
Kb; The Challenge.
Rm; Obviously there were family connections with other Bates in this list.

BECK. Later as, BECK & CO. [Cl, Im]. Ad; 21 Angel Hill, Tiverton, Devon.
Kb; Nk.
Rm; They were known active, Cr 1899-1900.

H. BECKWITH.   Ad; London (Rest of the Ad is Nk.
Kb; Nk.
Rm. An 1838 list of London Gm listed Beckwith, W. Andrews, Ad, 58 Skinner St, Snow Hill EC1.

JAMES BEDDOE. [Gs, Im]. Ad; Pembroke (Rest of Ad is Nk).
Kb; Nk.

BEENEY BROS (HAILSHAM) LTD.　　Ad; Hailsham, Sussex.
Kb; The Sussex.

ROBERT & EDMOND JOSEPH BELL. [Im]. Ad; 11 Church Square, Market Harborough, Leics. Also at, Bakehouse Hill, Kettering, Northants.
Kb; Bell's Special.

AUGUSTE EDOUARD LORADOUX BELLFORD. [Firearms inventor].
Ad; 16 Castle St, Holborn, London E6.
Kb; Nk.
Rm; It is thought that he may have had his name on shotgun ammunition.

ARTHUR W. BENNETT. [Im]. Ad; Market Place, Bideford, Devon.
Kb; The West Country.

G. W. BENNETT. [Gs]. Ad; Blackpool, Lancs.
Kb; Mullerite Red Seal, Mullerite Yellow Seal.
Rm; The above had additional tube printings.

S. W. BERRY.　　Ad; Woodbridge, Suffolk.
Kb; Un.

BEVAN.　　(Ad is not known).
Kb; The Dreadnought.

BEVAN & EVANS.　　Ad; Abergavenny, Monmouthshire (Gwent).
Kb; The Abergavenny Ace.

BEVAN & PRITCHARD. Ad; Abergavenny, Monmouthshire (Gwent).
Kb; The Abergavenny Ace.
Rm; Obvious connections to the previous entry with a name change.

C. G. BLACKADDER.　　Ad; Castle Douglas, Kirkcudbright (D & G).
Kb; The Black Douglas.

J. BLAIN. [Im]. Ad; Carlisle, Cumberland (Cumbria).
Kb; Nk.

BLAKE BROS. [Im]. Ad; Ross-on-Wye, Herefs (H & W).
Kb; The Wye Valley.

BLYTHE & WRIGHT. [Cl, Im]. Ad; Station Rd, Sheringham, Norfolk.
Kb; Nk.

EDWARD BOND. [Gm and rifle]. Ad; 25 White Hart St, Thetford, Norfolk.
Kb; Nk.
Rm; Most likely to have had his name on cartridges. He was known active,
Cr 1925-1929.

H & E. BOND. [Gm]. Ad; Market Place, Thetford. Also at, Diss, Norfolk.
Kb; Nk.
Rm; Nk if they had their names on cartridges. It is known that they sold
cartridges for both muzzle and breech loading. There has to have been family
connections with the entry above and with an entry in the Illustrated List
Section.

J. S. BOREHAM. [Gd and sports]. Ad; Colchester, Essex.
Kb; Excel Cartridge, Kynoch Witton Brand (Boreham's name on the stamping).
Rm; Business terminated in the late 1890's when taken over by Radcliffe.

C. BOTWELL.   Ad; Bungay, Suffolk.
Kb; Un.

BOWDEN.   Ad; Chagford, Dartmoor, Devon.
Kb; Un.

JOHN BOWEN.   Ad; Carmarthen, Carm (Dyfed).
Kb; Myrddin.

BOWERBANKS.   Ad; Penrith, Cumberland (Cumbria).
Also at, Kirkby Stephen, Westmorland (Cumbria.
Kb; Sure Killer, Un.

CHAS BOWTELL. [Im]. Ad; 14 St Mary's St, Bungay, Suffolk.
Kb; Nk (Frank Dyke loading).

BOZARD. Later as, BOZARD & CO.   Ad; 33 New Bond St. Also at,
4 Panton St, Haymarket, London SW.
Kb; Nk.
Rm; Their name has been seen on an over-shot card.

BRAND. [Cl with patent waddings]. Ad; Edinburgh, Midlothian. Also at,
Broxburn, West Lothian.
Kb; Nk.

BRIND GILLINGHAM. [Cl, Im]. Ad; Ock St, Abingdon, Berks.
Kb; Nk.

BRITT & SON. [Im]. Ad; 4 East St, Horsham, Sussex.
Kb; Nk.
Rm; Head stamping has been found.

R. BROADHURST. [Im and furnishing]. Ad; Smithford St, Coventry,
Warw (W. Midlands).
Kb; Eley's Special Smokeless.

S. BROADWAY & CO.   Ad; 84 Bridge St, Worksop, Notts.
Kb; The Dukeries Smokeless.

JOHN BROMLEY & CO. [Im]. Ad; Bridgnorth, Newport, Shifnal & Wellington,
Salop.
Kb; The Rabbit Special, Un.

E. J. BROWN & CO.   Ad; Rotherham, Yorks.
Kb; Kynoch Perfectly Gas-tight.

J. BROWN.   Ad; Morpeth, Northumberland.
Kb; Smokeless Cartridge, Special Cartridge.

BROWN & MURRY.   Ad; Haddington, East Lothian.
Kb; Special.
Rm; Their name has also been found on cartridge remains.

BUCK & CO. [Ga]. Ad; 11-12 St Andrew's Hill, London EC.
Kb; Shamrock Brand.

BUCKMASTER & WOOD. [Im]. Ad; 5 Market Place, Wokingham, Berks.
Kb; Un (Rabbit on case).
Rm; They were entered in trade directories, Cr 1899-1903. A 1907 directory showed just, Joseph Buckmaster at 5 and 7 Market Place.

BUDGE. [Gd and clockmakers]. Ad; Fore St, Callington, Cornwall.
Kn; Nk.
Rm; It is thought that they once sold their own cartridges.

J. U. BUGLER. [Gs, Im]. Ad; Ashford, Kent.
Kb; The National.

J. BULCOCK.   Ad; Burnley, Lancs.
Kb; Kynoch Ejector.

BULLEN BROS. [Im]. Ad; 32-33 Boscawen St, Truro, Cornwall.
Kb; Un.

GEORGE G. BULLMORE. [Id, Im]. Ad; 1 St George Rd, Newquay.
Also at, St Columb, Cornwall.
Kb; Un.

R. H. BUNNER. [Cl, Im]. Montgomery, Montgomeryshire (Powys).
Kb; Nk.
Rm; Their over-shot card has been seen. It is known that a loading machine was at one time installed on their premises.

WILLIAM BURGESS. [Gd and game]. Ad; Malvern Wells, Worcs (H & W).
Kb; Un 16 Gg pinfire (Burgess name on stamping).

BUTCHER.   Ad; Watton, Norfolk.
Kb; Un pinfire (Butcher.Watton. on white with red print over-shot card).

A. R. BUTLER. [Im and cycle agent]. Ad; Fore St, Bampton.
Also at, Tiverton, Devon.
Kb; Butler's Japs, The Special, The Wensledale.

BUYERS ASSOCIATION.   Ad; 72 Wigmore St, London W.
Kb; Un (Name on the head-stamping).

E. CALDER. [Gm]. Ad; 67 King St, Aberdeen, Aberdeens (Grampian).
Kb; County Favourite.

J. CALVERT.   Ad; Walsden, Near Todmorden, Yorks.
Kb; Eley Ejector (J. Calvert. Walsden, on stamping).

CARTRIDGE SYNDICATE LTD. [Cartridge sales].
Ad; 20-23 Holborn, London EC1.
Kb; The London, Spartan, Spartan Deep Shell.
Rm; Their cartridges were loaded by, Trent Gun & Cartridge at Grimsby, Lincs. It is possible that the two firms were linked. Their name was not on the boxes or the cartridges. This information has been taken from a 1930's advertisement.

F. G. CASSWELL. [Im]. Ad; Midsomer Norton, Radstock & Bath. Som (Avon).
Kb; Un.

CAVERHILL.   Ad; Berwick (Believed to be, Birwick-upon-Tweed, Northumberland.
Kb; Caverhill. Berwick. Has been seen printed on an over-shot card.

HERBERT CAWDRON. [Ammunition dealer]. Ad; The Butlands, Wells-Next-The-Sea, Norfolk.
Kb; The Holkham Cartridge.

J. CHAMERS & SON. [Im]. Ad; High St (North), Dunstable, Beds.
Kb; Nk.
Rm; Cartridge remains have been found by metal detecting.

R. CHAMBERS.   Ad; Bath, Somerset (Avon).
Kb; Nk.
Rm; This name has been seen printed on an over-shot card.

W. CHAPPELL. [Im]. Ad; 57 Queen St, Newton Abbot, Devon.
Kb; Nk.
Rm; I was told that they once sold their own cartridges.

CHARLES.   Ad; Wells, Somerset.
Kb; Nk.
Rm; 12 gauge cartridge remains have been found.

CHARLES BROS.   Ad; Market Place, Doncaster, Yorks.
Kb; The Don Smokeless.

Mrs S. CHARLES. [Im]. Ad; 46 High St, Stourport, Worcs (H & W).
Kb; Nk.
Rm; Head-stamping, Charles No 12 Worcester, has been found.

CLAPHAM.   Ad; Wigton, Cumberland, Cumbria.
Kb; Nk.
Rm; Several over-shot cards came to light printed, Clapham, Wigton.

CLARK & SON (DRIFFIELD) LTD.   Ad; New Humber St, Driffield, Yorks.
Kb; Nk.

FRANK CLARKE. [Im, cycle agent and pram maker].
Ad; Castle St, Thetford, Norfolk.
Kb; The Grafton, The Invincible.
Rm; Frank was active. Cr 1904-1965. Bond in Thetford also sold a cartridge called, The Invincible.

P. J. CLARKE.   Ad; Market Place & South St, Bourne, Lincs.
Kb; Nk.
Rm; Their name has been seen on a head-stamping.

CLATWORTHY. Later as, CLATWORTHY COOKE & CO. [Im].
Ad; Taunton, Somerset.
Kb; Ejector, The Pheasant Cartridge.

CLEMENT.   Ad; Abingdon, Berks (Oxon).
Kb; Nk.
Rm; This name was given to me as a possible for selling their own cartridges.

THOMAS CLEMITSON. [Im]. Ad; Haydon Bridge, Northumberland.
Kb; The Langley Castle.

R. CLIMIE & SO. [Gm]. Ad; Greenock, Renfrews (South Clyde).
Kb; Smokeless Cartridge, Special Cartridge.

F. K. CLISBY. [Cl, Gm]. Ad; Marlow, Bucks.
Kb; Special Loading.

THE CLUB CARTRIDGE CO LTD. [Ammunition sales].
Ad; 2 Pickering Place, London SW.
Kb; Clubs are Trumps.

BELL GAVIN CLYDE.   Ad; Clyde House, 46 Windsor Terrace,
Glasgow, Lanarkshire.
Kb; Nk.
Rm; Was known to have sold cartridges by Frank Dyke & Co and Mullerite.
There is possibility that he may have carried his name on some of them.

JOHN COLBY EVANS. [Im]. Ad; 4-5 Dark Gate, Carmarthen, Carm (Dyfed).
Kb; Un.

JOHN COLLINS LTD. [Caterers]. Ad; Drogheda, County Louth,
Republic of Ireland.
Kb; Nk.
Rm; I was once told of a cartridge by this firm.

COLTMAN.   Ad; Lutterworth, Leicestershire.
Kb; Nk.
Rm; In a stripped down cartridge was a wad with,' Cotman. Luttherworth' on it

COLTMAN & SON.   Ad; Stafford St. (Rest of Ad is Nk).
Kb; Nk.
Rm; A photograph of a cartridge would not divulge any more information.

H. CONYERS & SONS. [Gm]. Ad; 71 Middle St, Great Driffield. Also at,
Pocklington, Yorks. At one time at, 59 East St, Blandford Forum, Dorset.
Kb; The Express, Un.
Rm; This was a part of a family of Gm. John Conyers & Son, were also given the
Ad, 71 Middle St, and listed as, South Driffield. Also at, Market Place,
Pocklington. One of the sons named Frank was known to have loaded black
powder cartridges without brand names. Arthur Conyers was also related and
had his shop at 71 East St, Blandford Forum. I had him listed at being at, 3 West
St, Blandford Forum. (See in the Illustrated List section).

C. COOK & CO.   Ad; Bazaar, Leigh. (Rest od Ad is Nk).
Kb; Smokeless Cartridge.

THOMAS COOK.   Ad; Shepton Mallet, Somerset. Also at, Midsomer Norton & Bath, Somerset (Avon).
Kb; Nk.
Rm; Were known to have sold their own cartridges.

WILLIAM COOK.   Ad; Liverpool, Lancs (Merseyside).
Kb; Nk.
Rm; Stamping found on cartridge remains.

WILLIAMS COOMBES.   Ad; Frome, Somerset.
Kb; The Eclipse Cartridge (Kynoch's Pefectly Gas-tight).

GEO COOPER & SONS (PICKERING) LTD.   Ad; Market Place, Pickering. Also at, Kirbymoorside, Yorks.
Kb; The Noted Ryedale.

JOHN CORNISH. [Im]. Ad; 17-18 Fore St, Oakhampton, Devon.
Kb; The Noted Dartmoor, The Okement.

A. C. CORY. [Gd and ammunition]. Ad; Diss, Norfolk.
Kb; The Champion.

GEORGE COSTER & SON. [Gm]. Ad; 145 West Nile St, Glasgow, Lanarkshire (Strathclyde).
Kb; G. C. & S.

ADAM COTTAM.   Ad; Dalton-in-Furness, Lancs (Cumbria).
Kb; Kynoch's Perfectly Gas-tight.
Rm; A cartridge head with the stamping, COTTAM No 12 DALTON was found.

COTTIS & SON.   Ad; Epping, Essex.
Kb; Champion Smokeless.

B. & J. V. COULTAS. Ad; 91-92 Westgate, Grantham, Lincs.
Kb; Nk.
Rm; A 12 Gg cartridge remains was found with their name on the stamping.

THE COUNTRY GENTLEMENS ASSOCIATION. [Sporting Association].
Ad; Icknield Way, Letchworth, Herts.
Kb; The C.G.A. Improved Gastight, The C.G.A. Improved Waterproof Cartridge, The C.G.A. Keepers Cartridge.

COX & CLARKE. [Gm]. Ad; 28 High St, Southampton, Hants.
Kb; Fourten, Southampton Cartridge.

COX & MACPHERSON. [Gm]. Ad; 62 High St, Southampton, Hants.
Kb; Special.
Rm; Were known active, Cr 1907. Cox & Son were trading at that time from number 28 in the same street.

CRABTREE. [Cl, Gm]. Ad; Bridge St, Warrington, Lancs.
Kb; Daintith's Special.

THOMAS CRADDOCK. Later as, THOS CRADOCK & SON. [Im].
Ad; Leyburn, Yorks.
Kb; Nk.
Rm; Their name has been seen printed on an old style over-shot card.

ALFRED GEORGE CREBER. [Cl and sales]. Ad; Torcot, Menheniot, Liskeard, Cornwall.
Kb; The Creber Smokeless, The Creber Snap-shot Smokeless.
Rm; Alfred later founded the Cornwall Cartridge Works. This firm can be found in the Illustrated Cartridge List section.

G. CREIGHTON. [Gm]. Ad; 8 Warwick Rd, Carlisle, Cumberland (Cumbria).
Kb; Un.

CROSS BROTHERS LTD. [Sports outfitters]. Ad; 3-4 St Mary's St. Also at, Church St, Cardiff, Glamorgan.
Kb; The Cardiff.

C. G. CRUDGINGTON. [Gs, field sports]. Ad; 37 Broad St, Bath;
Kb; The Spa

H. & J. CUTLACK. [Im]. Ad; 11 High St, Eley, Cambridgeshire.
Kb; Nk.
Rm; Information given was that they once sold their own cartridges.

J. H. CUTTS.   Ad; Macclesfield, Cheshire.
Kb; The Special.

T. A. DADLEY. [Gm]. Ad; Stowmarket, Suffolk.
Kb; The Hard Hitting Cartridge.

THOMAS DAINTITH. [Gm]. Ad; 121 Bridge St, Warrington, Lancs (Ches).
Kb; Ejector, Eley Pegamoid, Special, Un.

N. S. DALL.   Ad; Chichester, Sussex.
Kb; Nk.
Rm; Cartridge remains have been found with Dall's name on the stamping.

WALTER DARLOW LTD. Later as, W. DARLOW & CO. [Gm, Im].
Ad; 27 Midland Rd, Bedford, Beds. Later at, 8 Orford Hill, Norwich, Norfolk.
Also at, Guildhall St, Cambridge, Cambs.
Kb; 20 Gauge, The Big Bag, The Castle, The Lightning, The Orford,
The Special, Special Gastight.
Rm; An 1894 directory listed Walter as Gm and Im.

T. DAVIES.   Ad; Llandyssul, Cardiganshire (Dyfed).
Kb; The Instanto Cartridge, Kynoch's Perfectly Gas-tight.

ALFRED DAVIS. [Gm]. Ad; 4 Bishopgate Churchyard, Old Broad St,
London EC2.
Kb; The Bishopgate.
Rm; He took over from John Blanch & Son. This firm is listed in the Illustrated section.

M. H. DAVIS & SONS. [Im]. Ad; Aberystwyth, Cardiganshire (Dyfed).
Kb; Nk.
Rm; Some time in the past I was given their name as having sold their own cartridges.

GEORGE H. DAW. [Central fire cartridge developer]. Ad; 67 St James's St. Also at, 57 Threadneedle St, London EC.
Kb; Un (Became known as The Daw Cartridge).
Rm; Daw's cartridges date from, Cr 1861. In 1866 George took Colonel Boxer and Messrs Eley Bros to court as he considered that between them they had made infringements on his patents. George lost his case and Eley Bros came out of it the better. Had he had won his case, then how different cartridge development may have involved in the British Isles.

A. DAWE. [Im]. Ad; Oakhampton, Devon.
Kb; Eley's Gastight Cartridge Case for Schultze Sporting Powder.

J. G. DEABILL.   Ad; Caelton, Nottingham, Nottinghamshire.
Kb; The Partridge.

HENRY DEAN. [Gm]. Ad; 71 North Rd, Durham, County Durham.
Kb; Un.

DENDY.   Ad; Saddler, Eastbourne, Sussex.
Kb; Nk.
Rm; Eley Bros 12 Gg stamping with Dendy name has been found.

ARTHUR DENNIS.   Ad; Geat Dunmow, Essex.
Kb; The Demon.

DESBOROUGH & SON.   Ad; Derby, Derbyshire.
Kb; The Dovedale Cartridge.

DEVON & SOMERSET STORES. [Ds, Im]. Ad; 245-246 High St, Exeter, Devon.
Kb; The Red Deer.

P. DICKER.   Ad; Odiham, Hampshire.
Kb; The Lightning Cartridge.

JOHN T. DICKINS. [Im]. Ad; 69 Bridge St, Northampton, Nothants.
Kb; Kynoch 5/8" Brass (Name on top card), Nobel Gas-tight Cartridge Case (Name on top card).

SIDNEY WILLIAM DIGBY. [Im]. Ad; 35 High St, Shaftesbury, Dorset.
Kb; The Demon.

DINWOODIE & NICHOLSON.   Ad; Thornhill, Dumfries,
(D & G. Dumphries & Galloway).
Kb; Eley Best Gas-tight Case.

FREDERICK M. DISS.   Ad; Colchester, Essex.
Kb; Kynoch Gastight (Diss's name on over-shot card).

E. DISTIN & SON. [Im]. Ad; 39 High St, Totness, Devon.
Kb; Demon Cartridge.

DIXON & CO. [Gm or Gs] Ad 34 Lozells Rd. Also at, Aston Common,
Birmingham, Warw (W. Midlands).
Kb; Special Hand Loaded (Kynoch Perfectly Gas-tight, Special Hand Loaded
Pigeon Cartridge.

DOBSON & ROSSON. [Gm]. Ad; 4 Market Head, Derby, Derbyshire.
Kb; Un.

G. DODD.   Ad; Perry Bar, Birmingham, Warw (W. Midlands).
Kb; Dodd's Calthorpe Cartridge.

W. G. DONANDSON.   Ad; Grantown-on-Spey, Morayshire (Highland).
Kb; The Triumph.

DOWNING.   Ad; Southwell, Nottinghamshire.
Kb; Schultze Co's Westminster (Downing's name on the over-shot card).

R. L. DUGDALE LTD.   Ad; 18 Friar Gate, Preston, Lancs.
Kb; Champion Smokeless, Mullerite Yellow Seal (Extra tube printings).

A. J. DUKES.   Ad; Rugby, Warwickshire.
Kb; Nk.
Rm; Cartridge remains have been found with Dukes head-stamping.

A. H. DUNCALFE. [Im and sanitary ware manufacturer].
Ad; 5 Merridale Rd, Wolverhampton, Staffs (W. Midlands).
Kb; Mullerite Yellow Seal (Extra tube printings).
Rm; The above Ad was taken from a 1932 directory.

THOMAS SMITH DUNCOMB. [Im]. Ad; 5 High St, Stamford, Lincs.
Kb; Un.
Rm; The cartridge seen had the name spelt as, T. S. Duncomb.

DYER & ROBSON. [Pyrotechnics]. Ad; London. (Rest of the Ad is Nk).
Kb; Superior, Very's Patent Signal Cartridge.

A. H. DYKES.   Ad; Stowmarket, Suffolk.
Kb; Un.

MARTIN DYMON.   Ad; Callington, Cornwall.
Kb; The Kit-Hill.

EASTMOND. Later as, EASTMOND & SON. [Im]. Ad; 10 Fore St,
Great Torrington, Devon.
Kb; Mullerit Smokeless (Extra tube printings).
Rm; They were known to have sold Eley Bros and Curtis's & Harvey's brands as
well as their own.

F. R. EDGAR.   Ad; Longtown, Cumberland (Cumbria).
Kb; Nk.

R. E. EDMONDS. [Im]. Ad; Stalham, Norfolk..
Kb; The Stalham, The Stalham Superior.

EDMONDS & WELLDON.   Ad; Rugby, Warwickshire.
Kb; Nk.
Rm; Cartridge remains have been found with the stamping,
EDMONDS & WELLDON No 12 RUGBY.

EDWARD BROS.   Ad; Bridlington, Yorks (Humberside).
Kb; Kn.

H. W. EGG. [Gm]. Ad; Piccadilly, London.
Kb; Nk.
Rm; A 12 Gg raised stamping head has been found through metal detecting.

WILLIAM ELLICOTT. [Cl]. Ad; Broad St, Launceston, Cornwall.
Kb; The Ellicott Cartridge (Kynoch's Perfectly Gas-tight).
Rm; An Advertisement for Ellicott, Launceston, was placed on the front cover of the very first "Shooting Times" publication dated, 9th September 1882.

J. ELLIS. [Sports Store]. Ad; Regal Sports Store, Oswestry, Shropshire.
Kb; The Regal Special Smokeless.
Rm; This firm stopped having their name on cartridges in 1947.

DAVID EMSLIE. Ad; Elgin, Morayshire (Grampian).
Kb; The Glen Moray, The Sniper.

ERSKINE. [Gm]. Ad; Newton Stewart, Wigtownshire (Dumfries & Galloway).
Kb; Nk.
Rm; Information gleaned was that they made their own cartridge cases, Cr 1890's. They closed down during the Fist World War.

EVANS & SON. Ad; Swansea, South Glamorgan.
Kb; Kynoch's Patent Perfectly Gas-tight, The Special.

CHARLES ALEX EVANS. [Im]. Ad; 134 High St, Burford, Oxfordshire.
Kb; The Cotswold Special Smokeless.

DAN EVANS. [Im]. Ad; Dursley House, Whitland, Carmarthen (Dyfed).
Kb; Ty-Gwyn.

T. EVANS & SON. Ad; Ashbourne, Derbyshire.
Kb; The Moorland.

THOMAS J. EVANS. Ad; Welshpool, Montgomeryshire (Powys).
Kb; Un.

J. W. EWEN. Ad; 45 The Green, Aberdeen, Aberdeens (Grampian).
Kb; The Ewen Special.

RICHARD FARMER. [Gm]. Ad; 12 North St, Leighton Buzzard, Beds.
Kb; The Ecel, Farmer's Challenge, Gastight.

GEORGE FARMILOE & SONS LTD. Ad; 34 St John's St, Smithfield, London EC.
Kb; Nk.
Rm; They were agents for F. Joyce & Co Ltd. It is not know if they had their own name on cartridges.

G. F. FARRELL & SONS. Ad; 23 High St, Chippenham, Wiltshire.
Kb; The Champion Special Smokeless.

FAWCETT. Ad; Kirby Lonsdale, Westmorland (Cumbria).
Kb; The Lunesdale Cartridge.

FAWCETT. Ad; Laxfield, Suffolk.
Kb; Nk.

FENWICK & SON. Ad; Stanhope, County Durham.
Kb; Nk.
Rm; Their name has been seen printed in red on a white over-shot card.

FERNIE. [Shooters supplies]. Ad; Aberfeldy, Perthshire (Tayside).
Kb; Hand Loaded.

FERRULES. Ad; The Arcade, Belfast, Northern Ireland.
Kb; Nk.

SAMUEL FIDDIAN. Ad; Stourbridge, Worcestershire (H & W).
Kb; The Enville Smokeless Cartridge.

C. F. FIELD. Ad; Pershore, Worcestershire (Hereford & Worcester).
Kb; The Eclipse Cartridge.

B. FINCH & SONS. Ad; 35 Bell St, Reigate, Surrey.
Kb; The Lone Flyer.

FISCHER BROTHERS.   Ad; Taunton, Somerset.
Kb; Nk.

HERBERT J. FISHER. [Im]. Ad; Bank St, Melksham, Wiltshire.
Kb; Mullerite Smokeless.

ARTHUR T. FITCHEW. [Gm]. Ad; 75 High St, Ramsgate, Kent.
Kb; Ecel, P.G.,

C. FLETCHER.   Ad; Leeds, Yorks. (Rest of Ad is Nk).
Kb; Kynoch's Perfectly Gas-tight.

FLINT. [Im]. Ad; Uckfield, East Sussex.
Kb; Un (Flint on over-shot card only).

RALPH FOORT. Ater as, R. FOORT & SON. [Im]. Ad; 19 Queen St. Later at, 47 Cornmarket St, Oxford, Oxfordshire.
Kb; The Dead Shot (In the name of R. Foort & Son).

FOSTER BROTHERS.   Ad; Church St, Ashbourne, Derbyshire.
Kb; Nk.
Rm; It was known that they once sold their own cartridges.

FOSTER LOTT & CO. [Ga]. Ad; The Ammunition Stores, Dorchester, Dorset.
Kb; Special Schultze Smokeless Cartridge.

E. J. FOY.   Ad; Minehead, Somerset.
Kb; Nk.
Rm; Their name has been seen printed on an over-shot card.

FOYS.   Ad; Athlone, Roscommon, Republic of Ireland.
Kb; Smokeless Cartridge.

JOHN FRASER.   Ad; Edinburgh, Midlothian.
Kb; Eley's Gastight Cartridge Case for S.S. Powder.

NORMAN FRASER. [Gs]. Ad; Station Rd, Churchdown, Glos.
Kb; Chosen.
Rm; Chosen was the abbreviated name for Churchdown. Only a small batch of these cartridges were produced. Norman was not related to any of the other Frasers in this cartridge list.

T. L. FREARSON. Later as, FREARSON & CO. [Im].
Ad; 9 Newmarket St, Skipton, North Yorks.
Kb; Nk.
Rm; A 12 Gg cartridge remains has been found with Frearson's name on the stamping.

FREENEY. [Im]. Ad; High St, Galway, County Galway, Republic of Ireland.
Kb; The Atom.

W. H. FRENCH. Later as, FRENCH & SON. [Im].
Ad; 8 Market Square, Buckingham, Buckinghamshire.
Kb; Nobel Explosives Co's Ejector (French's name on the over-shot card only).

E. FROST.   Ad; 6 Cowick St, St Thomas, Exeter, Devon.
Kb; The Devon Special Smokeless.

J. C. FROST.   Ad; Maldon, Essex.
Kb; Nk.
Rm; A 12 Gg cartridge remains has been found with J. C. Frost on the stamping.

S. C. FULLER. [Gun, cycle and sports dealer]. Ad; South St, Dorking, Surrey.
Kb; The Long Shot.
Rm; This firm was established in 1897.

FURLONG.   Ad; Saffron Walden, Essex.
Kb; Nk.
Rm; Their name has been seen on a 12 Gg stamping.

W. GALBRAITH. [Im, general furnishing and steel merchant].
Ad; 22 St Nicholas St, Lancaster, Lancashire.
Kb; Smokeless Cartridge (New Explosives Co Ltd loading).

J. & J. M. GALDING.   Ad; Monaghan, County Monaghan,
Republic of Ireland.
Kb; Surekill.

A. GALE. [Gm]. Ad; Barnstaple, Devonshire.
Kb; The Eclipse.
Rm; Most likely a family connection with Edward Gale who is listed in the Illustrated Section.

WILLIAM GARDNER. [Gm]. Ad; 6 High St, Chippenham, Wiltshire.
Kb; Warranted Gas-tight Cartridge Case.

M. GARNETT. Later as, M. GARNETT & SON.
Ad; Crampton Court. Later at, 31 Parliament St, Dublin, Republic of Ireland.
Kb; The Kilquick, The Pheasant, The Retriever, The Suredeath.
Rm; This firm later became, Garnett & Keegan at the same Ad.

ARTHUR GARRICK.   Ad; Sunderland, County Durham (Tyne & Wear).
Kb; The Sportsman.

FREDERICK WILLIAM GEORGE. [Im]. Ad; 3-4 Queen's Square,
High Wycombe, Buckinghamshire.
Kb; Eley Grand Prix Case.
Rm; He was known to have been active, Cr 1915.

W. GEORGE. [Im]. Ad; Ripon, Yorkshire.
Kb; Nk.

WILLIAM JOHN GEORGE. [Gm]. Ad; 192 Snargate St, Dover, Kent.
Kb; Un.
Rm; William was known to have been active, Cr 1908.

GERMANS. [Im]. Ad; Dulverton, Somerset.
Kb; Un.

GEVELOT & CO (LONDON). [French Am]. Ad; Queen Victoria St, London EC.
Kb; Ejector (Solid drawn brass).

GIFFORD.   Ad; Wincanton, Somerset.
Kb; Nk.
Rm; A 12 Gg cartridge remains has been found with Gifford, Wincanton on.

W. GILES.   Ad; Hay ? (I have no other Ad details).
Kb; Special Schultze Cartridge.

GILL & CO. [Im]. Ad; 5 High St, Oxford, Oxfordshire.
Kb; The Dead Shot.
Rm; They were known to have been active, Cr 1877.

JOHN H. Gill & SONS.   Ad; Leeming Bar, London.
Kb; The Sproxton.

C. GILLMAN & SONS. [Im]. Ad; Black Jack St, Cirencester, Gloustershire.
Kb; Nk.
Rm; They were known to have sold their own cartridges that were loaded for them by Page-Wood of Bristol.

R. W. GLANVILLE. [Gm or Gs]. Ad; 6 Wellington St, Woolwich, London SE.
Kb; Henrite Pigeon Cartridge..
Rm; Their name and Ad has been seen printed on a Kynoch's C.B. cartridge box. It has also been seen printed on an over-shot card that was loaded into a Luck's Explosives Ltd, Henrite Pigeon Cartridge.

GLOBEMASTER ARMS & AMMUNITION. [Ga].
Ad; 79 Oldstead Avenue, Hull, Yorkshire (Humberside).
Kb; Gamemaster.

G. E. GOLD. [Gm]. Ad; 9 Castle Mill St, Bristol, Gloucestershire (Avon).
Kb; The Popular.
Rm; This firm was known as active at the above Ad, Cr 1910.

CHARLES GOLDEN. [Gm]. Ad; Bradford, Yorkshire.
Kb; Un.

WILLIAM GOLDEN. [Gm or Gs and Im].
Ad; 6,8,10 & 12 Cross Church St, Huddersfield, Yorkshire.
Kb; Ejector, Kynoch Waterproof Cartridge Case.

C. E. GOLDING. [Im]. Ad; Watton, Norfolk.
Kb; The Wayland.
Rm; This cartridge was named after the local Wayland Wood. This was the legendary wood of the child's story, 'The Babes in the Wood'.

G. GRACE & SON. [Im and pistol makers]. Ad; 66-68 High St, Tring, Herts.
Kb; Un.

J. J. GRAHAM. [Gm or Gs]. Ad; Longtown, Cumberland (Cumbria).
Kb;Un.

J. & J. GRAHAM.   Ad; Sligo, County Sligo, Republic of Ireland.
Kb; Nk.

GRANDISONS.   Ad; London (Rest of the Ad is Nk).
Kb; Nk.
Rm; Cartridge remains have been found with Grandisons London on the head.

STEPHEN GRANT. [Gm].
Ad; 67A St James's St. Later at, 7 Bury St, St James, London SW1.
Kb; Instanter, Patent Gas-tight Cartridge, The R.P., Un pinfire.
Rm; Founded in 1866. Stephen later joined forces with Joseph Lang & Son.

GREENFIELD.   Ad; Storrington, Sussex.
Kb; Eley Ejector.

JAMES GREGSON [Gm or Gs]. Ad; 59 Penny St, Blackburn, Lancashire.
Kb; Eley's Ejector.

G. GREIGHTON.   Ad; 8 Warwick Rd, Carlisle, Cumberland (Cumbria).
Kb; Un.

CHARLES S. GRIFFITHS. [Gm or Gs]. Ad; Belmont Bridge, Skipton, Yorks.
Kb; The Craven.

W. J. GRIFFITHS. [Gm or Gs].
Ad; 87 Bridge St, Deansgate, Manchester, Lancashire (Great Manchester).
Kb; Eley's Gastight Case for E.C. Powder, Eley's Pegamoid.

WILLIAM GRIFFITHS. [Gm]. Ad; 5 Bridge St, Worcester, Worcs (H & W).
Kb; The Worcestershire Cartridge.

S. J. GRIMES. [Gun and ammunition depot]. Ad; Stamford, Lincolnshire.
Kb; The Champion Special, The Stamford Cartridge.

THE GUN SHOP.   Grantham, Lincolnshire.
Kb; Eley's Ejector (Name on over-shot card only).

GYE & MONCRIEFF. [Gm]. Ad; London. (Rest of the Ad is Nk).
Kb; Un.

J. B. HADDON. [Im]. Ad; Penzance, Cornwall.
Kb; Un.

HAGENS.   Ad; Rugby, Warwickshire.
Kb; Nk.
Rm; Their name has been seen printed on an over-shot card.

JOSEPH HAIGS. [Gm]. Ad; 49 St James's St, Portsea, Hampshire.
Kb; Nk.
Rm; He was known to have been active, Cr 1885. Several cartridge remains have been found with his name on the stampings.

CHRISTOPHER HALL. Later as, C. HALL & Co. [Gm].
Ad; Market Place, Knaresborough, Yorkshire.
Kb; Hall's Smokeless Castle, Un.

J. HALL.   Ad; Station Rd, Wigton, Cumberland (Cumbria).
Kb; Nk.
Rm; Both 16 and 12 Gg pinfire cartridge remains have been found.

T. HALL.   Ad; South Bank, (Rest of the Ad is Nk).
Kb; Eley Gastight Cartridge Case for Curtis's & Harvey's Smokeless Diamond Powder.
Rm; The limited information was taken from the over-shot card in the above mentioned cartridge.

M. HALPIN.   Ad; Shepperton, Middlesex (Surrey).
Kb; Nk.
Rm; Their name was seen on an Eley head-stamping.

HAMEYER & CO. [Im]. Ad; 4 Market St, Mansfield, Nottinghamshire.
Kb; Kynoch Nitrone (Their name was on the over-shot card only).

HAND BROTHERS. [Im]. Ad; High St, Odiham, Hampshire.
Kb; The Pheasant Smokeless.

F. G. HANDSCOMBE. [Im]. Ad; Bishops Stortford, Hertfordshire. Also at, Stansted, Essex.
Kb; Mullerite Yellow Seal (Extra tube printings).

JOHN ROBERT HANSON. [Gm and cycle]. Ad; 1 Cornhill. Also at, 244 High Bridge St. And also at, Hungate Passage, Lincoln, Lincolnshire.
Kb; Eley Bros pinfire (Hanson's name on the stamping).
Rm; He was known to have been active, Cr 1892-1908.

L. HANSON. [Gm]. Ad; 1 Cornhill, Lincoln, Lincolnshire.
Kb; Kynoch Grouse Ejector.
Rm; Has to have family connections with John Robert Hanson listed above.

HARDING BROTHERS LTD.   Ad; Commercial St, Hereford, Herfordshire (Hereford & Worcester).
Kb; The Rabbit Brand.

T. HARDING. [Im]. Ad; Wiveliscombe, Somerset.
Kb; Un (Harding's name on the over-shot card only).

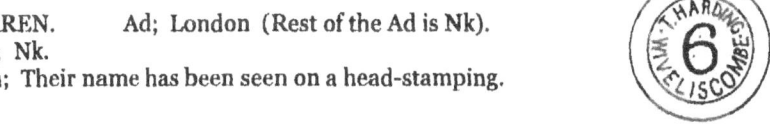

HAREN.   Ad; London (Rest of the Ad is Nk).
Kb; Nk.
Rm; Their name has been seen on a head-stamping.

J. HARPER. [Mg]. Ad; Fosseway Garage, Cropwell Bishop, Nottinghamshire.
Kb; Mullerite Yellow Seal (Extra tube printings).

PERCY J. HARPER. [Im]. Ad; 59 Market St. Also at, 44 Nantwich Rd, Crewe, Cheshire.
Kb; Harper's Invincible Smokeless.

HARPUR BROTHERS.   Ad; Waterford, County Waterford, Republic of Ireland.
Kb; Sure Shot Brand Cartridge.

H. HARRIS.   Ad; Leicester, Leics. (Rest of the Ad is Nk).
Kb; Un (Harris's name on the over-shot card only).

W. H. HARRIS & SON. [Im]. Ad; Totnes, Devonshire.
Kb; Harris's Lightning.

THOMAS HARRISON. [Gm or Gs]. Ad; 8 Bank St. Also, T. & W. HARRISON. And also, HARRISON BROTHERS. Ad; Carlisle, Cumberland Cumbria.
Kb; Un.
Rm; I do not know how to separate these Harrisons', but the above names have been seen on over-shot cards.

HARRISON & HUSSEY LTD. [Gm]. Ad; 41 Albemarle Street, London W1.
Kb; The Albemarle, The Grafton, Stafford Deep Shell.
Rm; Boss & Co Ltd, later traded from the above Ad.

ERNEST FREDERICK HART. [Im]. Ad; Clare, Suffolk.
Kb; Un.

HARTFORTH.   Ad; (Place and Ad is Nk).
Kb; Nk.
Rm; Remains have been found with the name Hartfoth on an Eley Bros stamping.

J. T. HARTWELL.   Ad; 5 Chapel St, Mayfair, London W1.
Kb; The Mayfair Cartridge.

HARVEY GUNS. [Ga]. Ad; Great Yarmouth, Norfolk.
Kb; Nk.

JOHN THOMAS HARWOOD. [Im, Cl]. Ad; St James's Square, Yarmouth, Isle of Wight.
Kb; Nk.
Rm; Information that I was given was that they once loaded shotgun cartridges.

HASTE.　　　Ad; Chelmsford, Essex.
Kb; Nk.
Rm; Un.

G. HAWKE & SON. [Im]. Ad; 37 Fore St, St Austell. Also at, Trafalgar Square, Fowey, Cornwall.
Kb; Mullerite Smokeless (Extra tube printings).

HAWKES & SONS LTD. [Im]. Ad; 32 East St, Taunton. Also at, Wiveliscombe, Somerset.
Kb; Hawk Brand.

HAYDENS.　　　Ad; 35 High St, ? (rest of the Ad is Nk).
Kb; Nk.

S. E. HAYWARD & CO LTD.　　　Ad; Tunbridge Wells, Kent. Also at, Crowborough, Sussex.
Kb; The New Special Smokeless.

T. HEATHMAN LTD.　　　Ad; 137 High St, Crediton, Devonshire.
Kb; Un (Kynoch Witton Brand Case (Heathman's name on the stamping).

HELY.　　　Ad; Dublin, Republic of Ireland. (Rest of the Ad is Nk).
Kb;Hely's Rlymax.

HELYAR & SONS. [Gm or Gs]. Ad; 93 Middle St, Yeovil, Somerset.
Kb; Un pinfire (Helyar on the stamping).

HELYER.　　　Ad; Ixworth, Suffolk.
Kb; Metalic.

HENDERSON.　　　Ad; Dundee, Angus (Tayside).
Kb; Kynoch Perfectly Gas-tight Cartridge for E.C. Powder.

W. HENSMAN. [Gm]. Ad; 19 Bridge St, Boston, Lincolnshire.
Kb; The Whirlwind.

W. G. HENTON. Later as, W. G. HENTON & SONS. [Im].
Ad; 204 High St, Lincoln, Lincolnshire.
Kb; Special Loading.

MRS EMILY HEWEN. [Im]. Ad; 12 Market St. Also at, Sheep St, Wellingborough, Northamptonshire.
Kb; Un.

HEWETT & SON.   Ad; Alton, Hampshire.
Kb; The Express.

HEYWOOD & HODGE.   Ad; Torrington, Devonshire.
Kb; The Reliable.

HICK FERNS & CO.   Ad; 32 Kirkgate, Otley, Yorkshire.
Kb; The Stoppum.

HICKLEY. [Im]. Ad; Farnham, Surrey.
Kb; Nk.

FREDERICK HICKS. [Gun and cycle agent]. Ad; 67 High St, Haverhill, Suffolk.
Kb; Special Loading.

E. & G. HIGHAM. [Gm]. Ad; 4 Chapel St. Also at, 4 Adelaide Buildings, Liverpool, Lancashire (Merseyside).
Kb; Gastight & Metal Lined, Patent Gastight Cartridge.

HOCKEY.   Ad; Brigg, Lincolnshire (Humberside).
Kb; Hockey's Woodcraft.

A. S. HOCKHELL. [Im]. Ad; Eccleshall, Staffordshire.
Kb; Un.

A. A. HODGSON. [Gm or Gs]. Ad; 27-29 Mercer Row, Louth, Lincs.
Kb; The Luda Cartridge.

J. HODGSON.   Ad; Lancaster, Lancashire.
Kb; The Lancaster.

FRANCIS HODGSON. [Gm or Gs]. Ad; 1 Market Place, Bridlington, Yorks.
Kb; Nk.
Rm; Kynoch made cartridge remains and also an over-shot card has been seen by Hodgson of Bridlington.

JESSE PARKER HODGSON. [Gm]. Ad; 27 Mercer Row, Louth, Lincs.
Kb; Nk.
Rm; Jesse was known active in Louth, Cr 1892-1908. By 1913 the above Ad was in the name of A. A. Hodgson.

R. C. HODGSON. [Gs and fishing tackle specialist].
Ad; 7 Queen St, Ripon, Yorkshire.
Kb; The Rapido.

R. T. HODGSON. [Im, Gs]. Ad; Station Bridge, Harrogate, Yorkshire.
Kb; The Harrogate.

JOHN HOLDRON. [Im]. Ad; Market St. Also at, Bath St, Asby-de-la-Zouch, Leicestershire.
Kb; The Rabbit.
Rm; John was known to have been active, Cr 1900-1928.

ISAAC HOLLIS. Later as, ISAAC HOLLIS & SON. [Gm or Gs].
Ad; Weaman Row, Lench St, Birmingham, Warwickshire (West Midlands).
Kb; Hollis' Special Blue Cartridge (By Royal warrant), Hollis' Special Green Cartridge (By Royal Warrant).

HOLME & ASH. [Im]. Ad; 3 Scarsdale Place, Buxton, Derbyshire.
Kb; The Peak Cartridge.
Rm; They were known to have been active, Cr 1904-1932. They were not listed in an 1881 trade directory. It is not known when the business terminated.

HOME'S.   Ad; 43 Friar St, Reading, Berkshire.
Kb; Home's Special Loading.

HORNE.   Ad; Reading, Berkshire.
Kb; Nk.
Rm; A 12 Gg head-stamping has been found. As yet, I have not been able to trace this firm.

HORRELL & SON. [Im]. Ad; 19 High St, Crediton, Devonshire.
Kb; Electric Smokeless Cartridge.

HORSLEY & SON.   Ad; Malton, Yorkshire.
Kb; Mullerite Smokeless.

HOWARD BROTHERS.   Ad; 240 St Ann's Rd, Tottenham, London W1.
Kb; Un.

WILLIAM HOWE & SONS LTD. [Im]. Ad; Shrewsbury, Shropshire.
Kb; Un (May have been called The Plough).

R. HOWSE,   Ad; South Hill, Fairford, Gloucestershire.
Kb; Nk'
Rm; A 16 Gg cartridge remains has been found with Howse name on the stamping and stating that the case was made in France.

C. S. HUDSON. [Im]. Ad; 34 Great Underbank, Stockport,
Cheshire (Great Manchester).
Kb; Un (Eley Bros case).

HUISH. [Im]. Ad; Porlock, Somerset.
Kb; Nk.
Rm; Information given was that cartridges were once loaded on their premises.

HULL CARTRIDGE CO LTD. Also known as, HULL CARTRIDGE. [Cl].
Ad; 58 De Grey St, Hull, Yorkshire (Humberside).
Kb; The Standard, Three Crowns, Un.
Rm; Developed Cr 1947 from the firm of Turners Carbides Ltd. They later loaded cartridges for many other firms. Most were crimped closed.

GEORGE HUME. [Gm]. Ad; 6 Loreburn St, Dumfries, Dumfriesshire (D & G).
Kb; Kynoch's Perfectly Gas-tight.

G. HUNT. [Mg]. Ad; Aston Hill Garage, Near Lewknor, Oxfordshire.
Kb; The Lewknor Cartridge.

HUNTER & MADDIL. [Gm]. Ad; 58 Royal Avenue, Belfast, Northern Ireland.
Kb; Un.
Rm; They were together in business, Cr 1890-1920.

HUNTER & VAUGHAN> [Gm or Gs]. Ad; 63 Broad St, Bristol, Glos (Avon).
Kb; Special Smokeless.
Rm; They were known to have been active, Cr 1908-1914, This firm was taken over by, Septimus Chamber & Co Ltd.

JAMES HUTCHINGS. [Gm]. Ad; 9 Bridge St, Aberystwith, Cardiganshire (Dyfed).
Kb; Kynoch Perfectly Gas-tight.

W. H. ICKE. [Im, general furnishing]. Ad; Smithford St, Coventry, Warwickshire (West Midlands).
Kb; Kynoch Perfectly Gas tight.

IDEAL.   Ad; London (Rest of the Ad is Nk).
Kb; Nk.
Rm; A 12 Gg cartridge remains has been found with Ideal. London, on the head-stamping.

ISLEY.   Ad; Salisbury, Wiltshire.
Kb; Un pinfire (12 Gg with reversed stamping. White over-shot card printed in red, ISLEY.SALISBURY.

DAVID IRONS & SONS. [Im]. Ad; Forfar, Angus (Tayside).
Kb; Un.

GEORGE IRVIN. [Im, ammunition dealer]. Ad; Penrith, Cumberland (Cumbria).
Kb; Nk.

JACKSON & SON.   Ad; Frome, Somerset.
Kb; See Rm.
Rm; A green cartridge by them was called The Selwood or Elwood or something similar.

ALFRED JACKSON. [Im]. Ad; Abergavenny, Monmouthshire (Gwent).
Kb; Un.

SAMUEL JACKSON. {Gm]. Ad; 7 Curch Gate, Low Pavement, Pepper St, Nottingham, Nottinghamshire.
Kb; Noted Brown Cartridge, Kynoch Patent Perfectly Gas-tight, The Nottingham Cartridge.
Rm; Sam was known to have been active, Cr 1881-1912.

THOMAS JACKSON & SON.   Ad; London. (Rest of Ad is Nk).
Kb; Nk.
Rm; Cartridge remains with reversed stamping has been found. Although it was 12 Gg, it carried no gauge size.

WILLIAM HENRY JANE. [Im and practice Gm]. Ad; Fore St, Bodmin, Cornwall.
Kb; The Bodmin.

JENVEY & CO. Later as, JENVEY & TITE.   Ad; Grantham, Lincolnshire.
Kb; Un.
Rm; A 20 Gg cartridge was stripped down That had a Jenvey & Tite over-shot card. Inside it contained a wad printed, Jenvey & Co. A 12 Gg cartridge remains has also been found with Jenvey on the stamping.

ROBERT BRINDLY JOHNSON. [Im and iron merchant].
Ad; High St, March, Cambridgeshire.
Kb; Un.

JONES & SON. [Im]. Ad; Oxford St. Also at, Gloucester St. Later at, 17 High St, Malmesbury, Wiltshire.
Kb;The Abbey.

F. JONES. [Im]. Ad; Ilfracombe, Devonshire.
Kb; The Champion.

ROBERT JONES. [Gm]. Ad; Monarch Gun Works, 42 Manchester St, Liverpool, Lancashire (Merseyside).
Kb; The Liver Cartridge, The Liver Smokeless.

J. THOMAS JONES. [Im]. Ad; Nott Square, Carmarthen, Carm (Dyfed).
Kb; The Majestic.

JOSLINS LTD.   Ad; Colchester, Essex.
Kb; Nk.
Rm; Cartridge remains have been found with Joslins name on an Eley Bros 12 Gg head-stamping.

WILLIAM JOWETT. [Cl, Im]. Ad; 3 Kingsbury, Aylesbury, Buckinghamshire.
Kb; The Kingsway.
Rm; At the end of shop loading, all unused cases were given to a museum.

D. & T. KEATING.   Ad; The Ammunition House, New Ross, County Wexford, Republic of Ireland.
Kb; Keating's Selected.

HON G. KEPPEL. [Pc]. Ad; Nk.
Kb; Kynoch Grouse Ejector (12 Gg with Keppel's name on the stamping).

HENRY ENGLISH KERRIDGE. [Gs, Im]. Ad; 184-185 King St, Great Yarmouth, Norfolk.
Kb; The Champion, The East Anglian, Un.

JOHN J. KILLEEN. [Cl]. Ad; Bridge House, Claremorris, County Mayo, Republic of Ireland.
Kb; Fur & Feather.

T. M. KINGDON & CO LTD. [Im, cycle agent]. Ad; 5 Market Place, Basingstoke, Hampshire.
Km; Eley's Gas-tight Cartridge Case (Kingdon's name on the stamping), The Encore, The Hampshire.

KING'S NORTON METAL CO.   Ad; King's Norton, Birmingham, Warwickshire (West Midlands).
Kb, Rm; The name 'Palma' was registered as, King's Norton Palma Cartridges.

THOMAS KIRKER. [Gm]. Ad; Belfast, Northern Ireland. (Rest of Ad is Nk).
Kb; Nk.

HUGH KIRKWOOD. [Im]. Ad; Lisburn, County Antrim, Northern Ireland.
Kb; The Clinker, Nobel's Sporting Ballistite.

H. KIRMAN. [Im]. Ad; Scunthorpe, Lincolnshire (Humberside).
Kb; Farmers Special.

J. N. KNIGHT. [Im]. Ad; Wells, Somerset.
Kb; Un.

KYNASTON BROTHERS. [Im]. Ad; Wem. Also at, Ellesmere, Shropshire.
Kb; Un.

LACE.   Ad; Market Place, Wigan, Lancashire (Great Manchester).
Kb; Lace's Smokeless Cartridge.

ARTHUR LACEY. Later as, LACEY & SON. [Im]. Ad; Bridge St, Stratford-upon-Avon, Warwickshire.
Kb; The Welcome Cartridge.

E. LAKER. [Im]. Ad; Montague St. Also at, 2 Buckingham Rd, Worthing, Sussex.
Kb; Nk.
Rm; This firms name has been seen printed on an over-shot card.

HENRY LAKER & SON. [Sports depot]. Ad; Billinghurst, Sussex.
Kb; The X.L. Special.

ROGER STANLEY LANAWAY. [Im]. Ad; Church Rd, Burgess Hill, Sussex.
Kb; Un.

LANE BROTHERS. [Im]. Ad; Marlborough St, Faringdon, Berks (Oxon).
Kb; The Eclipse, The O.B.H.

FRANK LANE & CO. [Im]. Ad; Marlborough St, Faringdon, Berks (Oxon).
Kb; Un (Pink paper tubes with a pheasant).
Rm; This firm was a continuation from Lane Bros. I have here listed them separately so as to show the Kb to each. They later became, Vale Agricultural and were based at Clanfield, Oxon. They then sold a crimp closed cartridge called 'The Vale' after the Vale of the White Horse that was loaded by the Hull Cartridge Co.

LANES. [Id]. Ad; Cheddar, Somerset.
Kb; The Cheddar Vale.

R. G. F. LAST.   Ad; Layer-de-la-Haye, Near Colchester, Essex.
Kb; Un.

LAWRENCE.   Ad; Durham, County Durham (Rest of Ad is Nk).
Kb; Nk.
Rm; Cartridge remains has been found with Lawrence, Durham, on the stamping.

J. F. LAYCOCK.   Ad; Wiseton, Nottinghamshire.
Kb; Eley Ejector.

LEATHAM.   Ad; Durham, County Durham.
Kb; Un.

LEAVER.   Ad; Weston-Super-Mare, Somerset, (Avon).
Kb; Nk.
Rm; This name has been seen on a head-stamping.

LEE.   Ad; Bishop's Stortford, Hertfordshire.
Kb; Nk.

W. R. LEESON.   Ad; Ashford, Kent. Also in, London (Ad Nk).
Kb; Eley Ejector (Name on over-shot card only), The Invicta.
Rm; Leeson was known to have been active, Cr 1896.

LEIGH & JACKSON. [Im]. Ad; Market Place, Witney, Oxfordshire.
Kb; Nk.
Rm; Cartridge remains have been found in 12 Gg with their name.

L. LePHERSONNE & CO. [Ammunition wholesalers].
Ad; 7-8 Old Bailey, London EC4.
Kb; Nk.
Rm; I am not sure but they may have placed their name on cartridges. They did market the following cartridges. Clermonite, F.N. (Fabrique Nationale D'Ames de Guerre), Lepco and Mullerite.

EDWIN GEORGE LEWIS. [Gs, wirelessengineer and cycle dealer].
Ad; London St, Basingstoke, Hampshire.
Kb; The Lewis Cartridge.
Rm; Edwin was known to have been active up until, Cr 1939. A 1911 directory listed a cycle agent in Reading Rd and also in May St. This firm was called, Lewis & Moss. There may have been a family connection.

F. LEWIS & SONS. [Im]. Ad; Great Dunmow, Essex.
Kb; Sharpshooter, Un.

GEORGE EDWARD LEWIS & SONS. [Gm]. Ad; 32-33 Lower Loveday St, Birmingham, Warwickshire (West Midlands).
Kb; The Express, The Keepers Cartridge, Pegamoid Case, The Premier.

J. D. LEWIS. [Cl, Im]. Ad; Narberth, Pembrokeshire (Dyfed).
Kb; Nk.
Rm; It is known that they once loaded cartridges.

RICHARD LEWIS. [Im]. Ad; 5 Lower St, Kettering, Northamptonshire.
Kb; Un (Pinfire, name on over-shot card only).

LICHFIELD AGRICULTURAL CO. [Id]. Ad; Market St, Lichfield, Staffs.
Kb; Un (Case by Eley Bros Ltd).

LIDDELL & SONS.   Ad; Haltwhistle, Northumberland.
Kb; Un.

LIGHTWOOD.   Ad; Bournmouth, Hampshire (Dorset).
Kb; Un (Blue Quality with stamping, LIGHTWOOD No 12 BOURNMOUTH and was loaded with an Eley Patent Wire Cartridge).

LIGHTWOOD & SON.   Ad; Price St, Birmingham, Warw (W. Midlands).
Kb; The Eeel.

LILLIE & DAY.   Ad; Macclesfield, Cheshire.
Kb; Un (Carried the E.B.L. shield trade mark).

LINCOLN JEFFERIES. Later as, LINCOLN JEFFERIES & CO. [Gm].
Ad; 121 & 140 Steelhouse Lane, Birmingham, Warwickshire (West Midlands).
Kb; The Lincoln Smokeless, Un.

LINCOLNSHIRE GUN AMMUNITION CO. (LINES GUN CO).
Ad; Brigg, Lincolnshire (Humberside).
Kb; Delivery, Glanford.

LINDSAY. [Im]. Ad; Perth, Perthshire (Tayside).
Kb; The Match Clayking Cartridge.

LINES GUN CO. (See, LINCOLNSHIRE GUN AMMUNITION CO).

LINSCOTT.   Ad; Exeter, Devonshire. (Rest of Ad is Nk).
Kb; Linscott's Champion.

H. C. LITTLE & SON. [Gm]. Ad; 14 Silver St, Yeovil, Somerset.
Kb; The Blackmoor Vale, The Spakford Vale, Un.

ALFRED THOMAS LITTLEFORD. [Gs, Im]. Ad; 2 Market Place,
Cirencester, Gloucestershire.
Kb; Specially Loaded by Improved Machinery.

CHARLES FREDERICK LIVERSIDGE. [Gm]. Ad; 29 Market St,
Gainsborough, Lincolnshire.
Kb; Ejector, Special Smokeless Cartridge.
Rm; Charles was known to have been active, Cr 1913.

LLOYD & LLOYD.   Ad; Newtown ? (Rest of the place and Ad is Nk).
Kb; Un (Name on over-shot card only).

C. H. LOCK.   Ad; 111 Long St, Atherstone, Warwickshire.
Kb; Lock's Special.

HENRY LONG & SONS. [Im]. Ad; Witney, Oxfordshire.
Kb; The Witney.

C. T. LOOK. [Im]. Ad; Eley, Cambridgeshire.
Kb; Nk.
Rm; Information guven was that they once sold their own brand of cartridges.

LOVERIDGE & CO. [Im, furnishing and hot water engineers].
Ad; 1-2 King St, Reading, Berkshire.
Kb; The Royal County Cartridge.
Rm; This firm was known active, Cr 1903. I once owned a cartridge box that had held Kynoch Nitrones. It was rubber stamped, Loveridge & Co.

S. LUCKES. [Gd]. Ad; Bridge St. Also at, Castle St, Taunton, Devonshire.
Kb; Taunton Demon.
Rm; This firm also had branches at, Langport, Washford, Wiveliscombe and St James Foundry.

LUCK'S EXPLOSIVES LTD. [Explosives manufacturers].
Ad; Leadenhall Buildings, London EC.
Kb; (See Henrite Explosives in the Illustrated Section).
Rm; Their works were at Stowmarket, Suffolk. Later also at Dartford, Kent. They were established in 1898 and were liquidated in 1906. Founded by A. Luck and L. Henry, they then later became, Henrite Explosives. The name 'Henrite' being registered to them in 1899.

LYNSCOTT.   Ad; Exeter, Devonshire. (Rest of Ad is Nk).
Kb; Nk.

MAC – Mc. These are both treated here as Mac. The next letter in the name determines the entry position.

ROBERT McBEAN. [Gm]. Ad; Stafford, Staffordshire. (Rest of the Ad is Nk).
Kb; The Challenge Cartridge.

McCARTHY BUCK & CO. [Gm]. Ad; 11-12 St Andrews Hill, London EC4.
Kb; Un (12Gg Pinfire).

McCOLL & FRASER. [Gm]. Ad; Dunfirmline, Fifeshire. (Rest of the Ad is Kn).
Kb; Un.

JAMES McCRIRICK & SONS. [Gm]. Ad; 72 Sandgate, Ayr,
Ayrshire (Strathclyde).
Kb; Nk.
Rm; Metal detecting has found their cartridge remains.

MACDOUGALL & CO.   Ad; Grantown-on-Spey, Morayshire (Highland).
Kb; The Bellheath, The Strathspey Challenge.

DUNCAN MACDOUGALL.   Ad; Oban, Argyllshire (Strathclyde).
Kb; The Lorne.

J. & J. McGALDING.   Ad; Monhagan, Republic of Ireland.
Kb; Sure Kill.

CHARLES MACGRGOR.   Ad; Kirkwall, Orkney, Orkney Islands.
Kb; Kynoch C.B. Cartridge Case (Extra tube printings).

McILWRAITH & CO.   Ad; Elgin, Morayshire (Grampian).
Kb; Un.

ALEXANDER MACINTOSH & SONS LTD. [Im].
Ad; 14 Market Hill, Cambridge, Cambridgeshire.
Kb; Special Smokeless Cartridge.

MACKENZIE & DUNCAN.   Ad; Brechin, Angus (Tayside).
Kb; The Dunmax.

CHARLES McLOUGHLIN. Later as, C. McLOUGHLIN & SON. [Gm and rifle].
Ad; 89 High St, Cheltenham. Also in, Cirencester, Gloucestershire.
Kb; Nk.
Rm; His cartridge remains have been found. Established 1815. In 1870, Charles was trading on his own. His sons name was added, Cr 1895-1902.

JOHN MACPHERSON. Later as, J. MACPHERSON & SONS. [Gm].
Ad; 24 Church St, Inverness, Inverness-shire (Highland).
Kb; The Bargate, Barrage Cartridge, The Clack, The Killer, The Royal, Un.

ROBERT MACPHERSON.   Ad; Kingussie, Inverness-shire (Highland).
Kb; The Badenoch.

JOHN McSORLEY. [Mg]. Ad; Omagh, County Tyrone, Northern Ireland.
Kb; Abercorn.

McVERY BROTHERS.   Ad; Cookstown, County Tyrone, Northern Ireland.
Kb; The Kill Quick.

MALLETT & SON. [Im]. Ad; 3,4 & 6 Victoria Place, Truro, Cornwall.
Kb; Nk.
Rm; In 1935 there was also an Im at, 6 Molesworth St, Wadebridge, Cornwall Trading as, Mallett & Son. Could have been the same firm.

MANN.   Ad; St Austell, Cornwall. (Rest of Ad is Nk).
Kb; Un (A brown cartridge with the stamping, MANN No 12 St AUSTELL.

MANNING.   Ad; Charmanton, Somerset.
Kb; Nk.

THOMAS GEORGE MANNING. [Im]. Ad; The Square, North Tawton, Devon.
Kb; Nk.
Rm; I was once told of a cartridge by him.

G. MARFELL.   Ad; Colwyn Bay, Denbighshire (Clwyd).
Kb; Nobel's Clyde (Extra tube printings).

J. STEWART MARK.   Ad; 114 South St, St Andrews, Fifeshire.
Kb; The Markmore.

MARRIAGE & CO.   Ad; Reigate, Surrey. (Rest of Ad is Nk).
Kb; Nk.
Rm; Cartridge remains have been found with their name on the stamping.

MARSHALL SONS & CO. [Steam and oil engine tractor manufacturers].
Kb; Tractor Start Cartridge (12 Gg but not a shotgun cartridge)
Rm; These are often included in cartridge collections.

J. H. MATIN & CO.   Ad; St John's ? (Rest of place and Ad is Nk).
Kb; Nk.
Rm; This name has been seen on 12 Gg cartridge remains. Corrosion has hid the rest of the Ad.

J. F. MASON. [Pc]. Ad; Eynsham Hall, Eynsham, Oxfordshire.
Kb; Eley Ejector (Mason's name on the stamping).

J. MATHER & CO. [Im, Id, Mg]. Ad; Castle Gate, Kirkgate & Bargate. Works at, Lombard St, Newark. Also in, King St, Southwell. And also at, Market Place, Bingham, Nottinghamshire.
Kb; Jas R. Watson & Co's Britannia Cartridge (Extra tube printings).

MATTERSON HUXLEY & WATSON.   Ad; Bishop St, Coventry, Warwickshire (West Midlands).
Kb; Nk.

MATTHEWS BROTHERS. [Im]. Ad; High St, Honiton. Also at, Lyme St, Axminster, Devonshire.
Kb; The Excelsior.
Rm; Their name has been seen on some Eley Bros Ltd head-stampings.

JAMES MATTHEWS. [Ga]. Ad; Ballymoney St, Ballymena, County Antrim, Northern Ireland.
Kb; Hawk, The Kingfisher, The Swift, The Wizard.
Rm; Established 1906. Numbers for Ballymoney St in my files were, 42 and 71-72. Most of their cartridges seen had stampings, SPECIAL No 12 SMOKELESS.

W. MAWBY & SON.   Ad; Birkenhead, Cheshire (Merseyside).
Kb; Nobel's Clyde (Extra tube printings).

MAWER & SAUNDERS. [Im]. Ad; The Square, Market Harborough, Leics.
Kb; The Demon Smokeless.

MAYES BROTHERS. [In, Id]. Ad; Wickford, Essex.
Kb; The Farmer's Favourite (It had the wording, 'A rabbit with every cartridge').

B. MEGGINSON.   Ad; Atherstone, Warwickshire.
Kb; Nk.
Rm; A 12 Gg cartridge remains has been found by them.

A. MELVILLE & SONS.   Ad; Dunbar, East Lothian.
Kb; Un.

METROPOLITAN GUNFITTING, COACHING & PRACTICE GROUNDS.
Ad; Neasden, London NW.
Kb; Joseph Lang & Son Ltd.

G. A. MIDGLEY. [Im]. Ad; Market Place, Winslow, Buckinghamshire.
Kb; Special Loading.

MILITARY EQUIPMENT STORES & TORTOISE TENTS CO LTD.
Ad; 7 Waterloo Place. Also at, 61 Pall Mall, London.
Kb; Un.

MILLS BROTHERS. [Im]. Ad; 137 High St, Crediton, Devonshire.
Kb; Kynoch C.B. Cartridge (Extra tube printings).

MINTO.   Ad; Wigton, Cumberland (Cumbria).
Kb; Nk.
Rm; I was told that they once sold their own cartridges.

WILLIAM MOORE. Later became, W. MOORE & GREY. [Gm].
Ad; 11 The Arcade, Aldershot, Hants. Also at, 156 Piccadilly, London W1.
Kb; Kynoch Grouse Ejector, Un (Pinfire).

S. MORELAND. [Gd]. Ad; Northwich, Cheshire.
Kb; Special Smokeless.

MORETON.   Ad; Helston, Cornwall.
Kb; The Popular Cartridge.

J. P. MORETON & CO.   Ad; Colonnade Passage, Birmingham, Warwickshire (West Midlands).
Kb; Smokeless Waterproof.

MORGAN. [Gd]. Ad; Wem. Also at, Whitchurch, Shtopshire.
Kb; Special Smokeless Cartridge.

MORREYS.   Ad; Holmes Chapel, Near Middlewich, Cheshire..
Kb; Morreys Special.

H. M. MORRIS.   Ad; Rescent Rd, Burgess Hill, West Sussex.
Kb; Specially hand-loaded in England.

H. MORTIMER. [Im]. Ad; 50 Boutport St, Barnstaple, Devonshire.
Kb; The Club, Club Smokeless.

GEORGE PERCY MORTON & SON. [Im].
Ad; 22 High-Causeway, Whittlesey, Cambridgeshire.
Kb; The Killer.

C. MOTTERM. [Im]. Ad; Uttoxeter, Staffordshire.
Kb; Nk.

MOULTON & BENNETT.   Ad; Eye ? (Location Nk, possibly in Suffolk).
Kb; Un Eley Blue Quality Case (Moulton & Bennett on the over-shot card only).

MULLER & CO. [Cartridge agents}. Ad; Horseshoe Yard, Mount St, London W1. Also at, Winchmore Hill, Middlesex.
Kb; Clermonite, Mullerite, Negro.
Rm; This firm was founded in 1901 in Mount St, to market Mullerite cartridges in the UK. They made a move to Winchmore Hill in 1903, only to close down in 1905. Martin Pulvermann & Co Ltd, then took over the Mullerite agency. See Mullerite Cartridge Works, in the Illustrated Section.

W. H. MURCH.   Ad; 66 High St, Southwold, Suffolk.
Kb; Nk.

DAVID MURRAY & SON. [Gm]. Ad; 23 St David's St, Brechin, Angus (Tayside).
Kb; The Reliable.

T. NAUGHTON & SONS LTD. [Im, furnishings and sports].
Ad; Shop St, Galway, County Galway, Republic of Ireland.
Kb; The Blazer, The Connaught.
Rm; They were established in 1891. Their phone number was, Galway 63.

CLEMENT NAYLOR LTD. [Gm]. Ad; Bridge St, Snighill. Also at, 34 West Bar & 6 Woodhead Rd, Sheffield, Yorkshire.
Kb; Naylor's Cannot Be Beaten.

NESTOR BROTHERS.   Ad; 28 O'Connell St, Limerick, County Limerick, Republic of Ireland.
Kb; The Shannon.

WILLIAM NEWMAN & SON.   Ad; High St, Haverhill, Suffolk.
Kb; Nk.
Rm; Their name has been found on cartridge remains.

J. H. NICHOLAS. [Im]. Ad; Thirsk, Yorkshire.
Kb; The Express.

NICHOLS. [Im, Cl]. Ad; Porlock, Somerset.
Kb; Nk.
Rm; I have been told that cartridges were once loaded on their premises.

J. O. & R. W. NICOLL. [Country outfitters]. Ad; Aberfeldy, Perthshire (Tayside).
Kb; Nk
Rm; Printed on some of their cartridges were the wording, 'Shooters best hand made waterproof tights made to measure'.

NIXON & NAUGHTON. {Gm]. Ad; Newark, Nottinghamshire.
Kb; Nk.

NORMAL IMPROVED AMMUNITION CO. [Am]. Ad; Hendon, London NW4.
Kb; 410 Cartridge, Hendon, Keepers Normal, Light Blue, Normal,
Normal Midget, Pegamoid, Pigeon Cases, Super Nimrod.
Rm; This firm seems to be an intermediate between the Normal Powder Co and
the New Normal Ammunition Co Ltd. These later two here mentioned are listed
in the Illustration Section.

NORMAL POWDER SYNDICATE LTD.
Ad; 38-39 Parliament St, London SW.
Kb; Nk.
Rm; They sold the Normal Powder Co's goods. It is Nk if they had their own
name placed on a cartridge.

NORRINGTON.   Ad; Chard, Somerset.
Kb; Norrington's Special Chardian.

J. H. B. NORTH & SON. [Id]. Ad; Stamford, Lincolnshire. Also at,
Broadway, Peterborough, Northamptonshire (Cambridgeshire).
Kb; North's Universal.
Rm; Cartridges were loaded for them by, G. L. Woods, of Ovington, Norfolk.
Closures may have been crimp or rolled turn-over.

J. E. NOTT & CO. [Sports depot]. Ad; Brecon. Also at, Llandridod Wells,
Radnorshire (Powys).
Kb; Un.

JOHN ODELL. Later as, ODELL BROTHERS. [Cl, Im].
Ad; 13 High St, Newport Pagnell, Buckinghamshire (Milton Keynes).
Kb; Nk.
Rm; Established well over 200 years. In an 1877 directory the firm was listed as
John Odell. Several times I had called in on this shop which was then run by
two aged gentlemen. I never managed to come away with a cartridge that was
loaded for themselves, but I never failed in coming away with a cartridge that
they had loaded for another firm.

HERBERT O'LEE.   Ad; Bishop's Stortford, Hertfordshire.
Kb; The Sharpshooter.

OLIVER & CO. [Gm]. Ad; Hull, Yorkshire (Humberside).
Kb; The Estate.

JOSEPH PHILLIP OSBORN. [Cartridge sales]. Ad; The Golden Padlock, Daventry, Northamptonshire.
Kb; The Danetre Cartridge.

CHARLES OSBORNE & CO LTD. [Gm including punt guns]. Ad; 12, 13, 14 Whittal St. Also at, Sandgate St, Birmingham, Warw (W. Midlands). And also at, 2 Great Scotland Yard, London SW.
Kb; Un, One and three quarter inch punt gun cartridge.

WALTER OTTON. Later as, W. OTTON & SONS. [Im]. Ad; Exeter, Devon.
Kb; The Devon, The Express, The Long Tom.

OVERSEAS BUYING AGENCY.   Ad; Carmelite House, London. (Rest of the Ad is Kn).
Kb; The Overseas Cartridge, Daily Mail (Printing as on the newspaper heading on the case wall).
Rm; The stamping on the Daily Mail was, WILKINSON No 12 PALL MALL.

PALMER SON & CO.   Ad; Barnet, Hertfordshire (Great London).
Kb; Eley Ejector, Rocketer.

W. G. PALMER. [Gm]. Ad; Rochester, Kent. (Rest of the Ad is Nk).
Kb; The Champion Smokeless.

W. PALMER JONES (GUNS). (This firm is listed in the Illustrated Section as, W. P. JONES).

PALMER & TARR. [Id]. Ad; Minhead, Somerset.
Rm; For Kb, see, J. GLIDDON & SONS, in the Illustrated Section. Also see, WILLIAM TARR & SONS, in this section cartridge list.

PARAGON GUN SPECIALISTS.   Ad; 43 Ann St, Belfast, Northern Ireland.
Kb; The Crown, The Invincible, The New Era, Paragon Special, Special.

J. PARKINSON.   Ad; Dublin, Republic of Ireland. (Rest of the Ad is Nk).
Kb; Un.

F. PARSONS. [Im]. Ad; Littlehampton Rd, Worthing, West Sussex.
Kb; The High Down.

S. PAXTON & CO.   Ad; High St, Stokesley, Yorkshire.
Kb; Eley Deep Shell (Eley-Kynoch I.C.I. case with name on over-shot card only).
Rm; Was known to have been active, Cr 1937.

G. & J. PECK LTD. [Im]. Ad; 43 High St, Ely, Cambridgeshire.
Kb; Un or Nk.
Rm; A cartridge seen had an Eley Bros Ltd maroon coloured paper tube. They were known to have been active, Cr 1929.

PERRINS & SON.   Ad; Worcester, Worcs (H & W). (Rest of Ad is Nk).
Kb; Eley's Ejector (Perrin's name on the head-stamping).

S. PERROTT. [Im, Sm]. Ad; Patent Gastight Cartridge (Overprint on a 14 Gg Eley Bros Ltd case for Schultze gunpowder).

C. PLAYFAIR & CO.   Ad; Aberdeen, Aberdeenshire (Grampian).
(Rest of the Ad is Nk).
Kb; Ejector.

W. H. POLLARD.   Ad; London. (Rest of the Ad is Nk).
Kb; Nk.
Rm; Cartridge remains have been found by metal detecting with the stamping, W.H.POLLARD No 12 LONDON.

JOHN EDWARD PONTING. [Cl, Im]. 43,44 & 46 High St. Also at, Garsdon, Malmesbury, Wiltshire.
Kb; Nk.
Rm; I had been told in their shop that they once loaded their own cartridges.

POOLE BROTHERS.   Ad; Taunton, Somerset. (Rest of the Ad is Nk).
Kb; Mullerite Yellow Seal (Extra tube printings).
Rm; I was told that they were an agent for Mullerite cartridges.

WILLIAM POOLE. [Im]. Ad; Market Hill, Haverhill, Suffolk.
Kb; Nk.
Rm; It is known that they sold the products of the, New Explosives Co Ltd.

R. C. POTTER. Later as, POTTER & CO. [Gs]. Ad; 1 Cornmarket, High Wycombe, Buckinghamshire.
Kb; Un (Centre and pinfire).
Rm; They were known as active, Cr 1915.

POWELL.   Ad; Tunbridge Wells, Kent. (Rest of the Ad is Kn).
Kb; Powell's Special.

T. POWELL & CO LTD. [Explosives merchants and shooting ground].
Ad; Bemberton, Salisbury, Wiltshire.
Kb; Eley's Gas-tight Cartridge Case for Walsrode Powder (Powell's name on the head-stamping).

ALBERT PRATT. [Im and ammunition dealer]. Ad; 27 High St, Knaresborough, Yorkshire.
Kb; The Fysche.

THOMAS PRENTICE & CO.   Ad; Stowmarket, Suffolk. (Rest of Ad is Nk).
Kb; Patent Gun Cotton Cartridge (Pinfire).

PRESTON & DISTRICT FARMERS TRADING SOCIETY LTD.
Ad; Preston, Lancashire. (Rest of the Ad is Nk).
Kb; Farmers General Purpose.

PRESTWICH & SONS.   Ad; Longridge, Lancashire.
Kb; Eley's E.B. Nitro Cartridge Case (Prestwich name on the over-shot card only).

W. H. PRICE.   Ad; Chester St, Hold. ? (See Rm below).
Kb; The Champion.
Rm; I do not know a place named Hold. A mistake may have been given to me, or, it may have been an abbreviation. Perhaps some wording was missing from a cartridge.

W. PROUT. [Mg, also in cycles and ammunition}. Ad; Launceston, Cornwall.
Kb; Un.

HENRY PULLAN. [Cycle and Gm]. Ad; Linden Cycle & Gun Works, Castle St, Cirencester, Gloucestershire.
Kb; The V.W.H. (Vale of the White Horse).

W. J. PULLEN LTD.   Ad; Sittingbourne, Kent. (Rest of the Ad is Nk).
Kb; Yellow Seal Mullerite.

R. RAMSBOTTOM. [Sports Store]. Ad; Manchester, Lancs (Gt Manchester).
Kb; Schultze, The Sudden Death Smokeless Cartridge Mk II.

M. RAY. [Gm]. Dartford, Kent. (Rest of the Ad is Nk).
Kb; Un.

REDMAYNE & TODD.   Ad; Nottingham, Notts. (Rest of the Ad is Nk).
Kb; Un.

REDMONDS.   Ad; Stalham, Norfolk. (Rest of the Ad is Nk).
Kb; Nk.

E. M. REILLY & CO. [Gm}. Ad; 277 Oxford St. Also at, 16 New Oxford St, London WC.
Kb; Eley's Gas-tight Cartridge Case for Schultze Sporting Powder (Reilly's name on the head-stamping), The Harewood, Un, Un pinfire 15 Gg (Reilly's name on the head-stamping).
Rm; All cartridges by E. M. Reilly & Co, are prior 1900. They were at 277 Oxford St, Cr 1890. Another Ad that I was given for them was at, 205 and 295 Oxford St.

JOHN REYNOLDS.   Ad; Cullompton, Devonshire.
Kb; Champion, Culm Vale, Un.

RHODES.   Ad; Scarborough, Yorkshire. (Rest of the Ad is Nk).
Kb; Eley Ejector (Rhodes name on the over-shot card only).

F. J. RICHARDS.   Ad; Taunton, Somerset. (Rest of the Ad is Nk).
Kb; Kynoch's Patent Perfectly Gas-tight.
Rm; This firm stopped trading in 1866.

GEORGE B. RICHARDSON. [Gm or Gs]. Ad; 18 Bridge St, Cardiff, Glamorgan.
Also at, Benjamin Bank, Barnard Castle, County Durham.
Kb; Nulli Secundus.
Rm; There could well have been family connections with, William G. Richardson. See, WILLIAM G. RICHARDSON in the Illustrated Section.

G.`M. RICHARDSON.   Ad; Dumfries, Dumfries-shire (Dunfries & Galloway). (Rest of the Ad is Nk).
Kb; Buccleuch, Criffel, Ideal.

RICHARDSON & CLINGEN.   Ad; Enniskillen, Managh, Northern Ireland.
Kb; The Killem.

RICKARBY & PARTNER. (A. G. RICKARBY). [Gm or Gs]. Ad; 37A Finsbury Square, London EC2. Also at, 12-16 New Rents, Ashford, Kent.
Kb; Nk.
Rm; They were U.K. agents for the American, United States Cartridge Co's, U.S. Defiance. It is Nk if they ever had their name on a cartridge.

BEN RIGBY. [Game dealer]. Ad; Malden, Essex.
Kb; Un.

R. L. AMMUNITION CO.   Ad; 27 Upper Marylebone St, London W1.
Kb; Un (One and a half inch shell 'powder carrier').

H. E. ROBERSON. [Im, Gd and ammunition]. Ad; High St, Towcester, Nothamtonshire.
Kb; The Towcester.

EDGAR ROBERTS. [Gm]. Ad; 5 & 141 Steelhouse Lane. Also at, 22 Weaman St, Birmingham, Warwickshire (West Midlands).
Kb; The Forward Cartridge, The Reliance.

H. P. ROBERTS. [Im]. Ad; Ottery St Mary, Devonshire.
Kb; Ottervale, Eley Yeoman (Extra tube printings).

H. W. ROBERTS & CO.   Ad; Rhyl, Flintshire (Clwyd).
Kb; Kynoch Patent Grouse Ejector, Special Blend.

T. H. ROBERTS & SON. [Cl, Im]. Ad; Parliament House, Dolgelley, Merionethshire (Dolgellau, Gwynedd).
Kb; Un.

ROBERTSON.   Ad; Peebles, Peebles-shire (Borders). (Rest of Ad is Nk).
Kb; Un or Nk.
Rm; A cartridge seen had a KYNOCH BIRMINGHAM head-stamping.

ALEXANDER ROBERTSON & SON. [Gm or Gs, Im]. Ad; Bridge St, Wick, Caithness-shire (Highland).
Kb; Eley Gas-tight Case, The Expert, Special Smokeless.

ROBINSON BROTHERS. [Im]. Ad; Loftus, Yorkshire (Cleveland).
Kb; Un.

H. ROBINSON & CO. [Gs, Im and cycle makers]. Ad; Bridgnorth, Salop.
Kb; The Castle, Special Smokeless.

ROBERT ROPER, SON & CO LTD. [Gm]. Ad; 39 Sheaf St. Also at, 8 South St, & 9 Exchange St, Sheffield, Yorkshire.
Kb; Eley's Gas-tight Cartridge Case, The Hallamshire Cartridge, Kynoch's Patent Perfectly Gas-tight.

R. ROUS. [Mg]. Ad; Beyton, Suffolk.
Kb; Un.

ROWE & CO.   Ad; Aylesbury, Buckinghamshire. (Rest of the Ad is Nk).
Kb; Hall's Cannonite (Coarse Grain).

W. W. ROWE. [Gm]. Ad; 62 High St, Barnstaple. Also at, 63 Winner St, Paignton, Devonshire.
Kb; Nk.
Rm; I have been told of cartridges by them. There was also listed a Gm, James Rowe as being at, 62 High St, Barnstaple, at some other time.

ROBERT ROWELL & SON. [Im, engineers and brass founders].
Ad; 7 High St, Chipping Norton, Oxfordshire.
Kb; Sure Killer.

ROYS. [Im]. Wroxham, Norfolk.
Kb; Roys De Luxe, Roys Rabbit Cartridge.

ALEX RUTHERFORD. [Sports store]. Ad; Sportsmans Repository, Blackwellgate, Darlington, County Durham.
Kb; The Champion.

W. M. E. E. RUTHERFORD. Ad; 9 & 11 Walkergate, Berwick-upon-Tweed, Northumberland.
Kb; Un.

RUTT & CO. Ad; 13 Bridge St, Northamton, Northamptonshire.
Kb; Nk.
Rm; There may have been a family connection with, Alfred H. Rutt the Gm who is listed in the Illustrated Section.

R. D. RYDER. [Im]. Ad; Rhayder, Radnorshire (Powys).
Kb; Ryder's True Blue.

SANDBROOK & DAWE. [Cl, Im]. Ad; Crane St, Pontypool, Mon (Gewnt).
Kb; Nk.
Rm; Cartridges had been once loaded on their premises.

SANDERS. [Pc]. Ad; Plymtree, Ford Moor, Devonshire.
Kb; Nk.
Rm; I was given this Ad but with no cartridge details.

JOHN HENRY SANDERS. [Im]. Ad; Combe Martin, Devonshire.
Kb; The Mighty Atom Cartridge.

SANDLEFORD PRIORY ESTATE. [Pc]. Ad; Sandleford, Near Newbury, Berkshire.
Kb & Rm; Printed over-shot cards were purchased. The head keeper after a shoot collected up empty cases and then reloaded using these printed top cards.

SARSON.   Ad; Aylesbury Bucks. (Rest of the Ad is Nk).
Kb; Nk.
Rm; Cartridge remains have been unearthed with Sarson on the stamping.

G. E. SAUL.   Ad; Lymington, Hampshire.
Kb; Nk.
Rm; This name has been seen on an over-shot card.

E. F. SAUNDERS. [Im]. Ad; 53 South St, Chichester, Sussex.
Kb; The Golden Pheasant.

JOHN A. SCOTCHER. Later as, J. A. SCOTCHER & SON. [Gm].
Ad; 4 The Traverse. Also at, Market Hill, Bury St Edmunds, Suffolk.
Kb; Eley's Gas-tight Cartridge Case for Schultze Gunpowders, The Invincible, Special Smokeless Cartridge.
Rm; This business was taken over in 1913 by Henry Hodgson. This then makes all of Scotcher cartridges prior to that year.

SCOTT & SARGEANT. [Im]. Ad; 26 East St, Horsham, Sussex.
Kb; The Horsham Special, The Ironmonger.

SERCOMBE.   Ad; Bovey Tracey, Devonshire.
Kb; Un pinfire (Sercombe's name on the over-shot card only).

J. G. SEWARD. Later as, SEWARD & CO. [Im].
Ad; Eastbrook, Wimborne, Dorset.
Kb; Nk.
Rm; Their name has been seen on a stamping of cartridge remains.

F. A. SHARP & SON. [Im]. Ad; 69 High St, Poole, Dorsetshire.
Kb; Sharp's Express.

SHARPLAND BROTHERS.   Ad; Wellington. / (Rest of the Ad is Nk).
Kb; The Wellington Cartridge.

FRANCIS B. SHUFFERY. Later as, SHUFFERYS LTD. [Im].
Ad; 245 Stafford St. Also at, 20 Caldmore, Walsall, Staffs (W. Midlands).
Kb; The Beacon.
Rm; Many of these Beacon cartridges were found under a shop floor.

S. W. SILVER & CO. Ad; London. (Rest of the Ad is Nk).
Kb; Nk.
Rm; Cartridge remains were found in India with the head-stamping,
S. W. SILVER & Co No 12 LONDON.

SIMPSON. Ad; Piccadilly, London W1.
Kb; Nk.

SKELTONS LTD. Ad; Warrington, Lancashire (Cheshire).
Kb; Nk.
Rm; Their name has been seen on a head-stamping.

SKEMPTONS. Ad; Bovey Tracey, Devonshire.
Kb; Nk.
Rm; Their name has been seen printed on an over-shot card.

SLATER. Ad; Warwick St, Leamington Spa, Warwickshire.
Kb; Nk.

SLINGSBY. Ad; Leeds, Yorkshire. (Rest of the Ad is Nk).
Kb; Un (Their name was on the head-stamping and over-shot card).

SAMUEL SMALLWOOD. [Gm]. Ad; 12 High St. Also at, Milk St,
Shrewsbury, Shropshire.
Kb; Smallwood's Challenge, Smallwood's Kleankiller, The Nitrone Cartridge.

R. B. SMART. Ad; Atherstone, Warwickshire.
Kb; Yellow Seal Mullerite (Extra tube printings).

BARTON SMITH. [Id, Im]. Ad; Sligo, County Sligo, Republic of Ireland.
Kb; Nulla Nisi Aroua The Unicorn (Has a, ELEY 12 12 KYNOCH stamping,
Nulla Nisi Aroua The Vogue.
Rm; Established in 1878. The Vogue was named after the Garravogue River.
All items that were made for them were stamped with a Unicorn.

CHARLES HUBERT SMITH & CO. [Gm]. Ad; 123 Steelhouse Lane,
Birmingham, Warwickshire (West Midlands).
Kb; The Abbey, The Invincible.

DUNCOMB SMITH. [Im]. Ad; 5 High St, Stamford, Lincolnshire.
Kb; Nk.
Rm; Spelling was as, T. S. Duncomb Smith on the seen cartridge.

E. H. SMITH.   Ad; Northallerton, Yorkshire.
Kb; Un (A woodcock was portrayed on the case wall).

GEORGE SMITH. Later as, G. SMITH & SON. [Gm].
Ad; 4 Travies Inn, Holborn, London.
Kb; Un pinfire (The stamping had raised wording).

SMOKELESS POWDER CO LTD. [Gunpowder manufacturers].
Ad; Dashwood House, New Broad St, London EC. Works at, Barwick, Herts.
Kb; Smokeless S.S. Sporting.
Rm; They were known to have been active up to, Cr 1896.

SMOKELESS POWDER & AMMUNITION CO. (S. P. & A. Co.). [Am, and powder]. Ad; 28 Gresham St, London EC.
Kb; Ejector, Un.
Rm; It was formed in 1887 to market its S.S. gunpowder. In 1898 the firm was terminated. It is worth noting the similarities of the logo with those of three other firms. They are, The Smokeless Powder Co, Ltd. The Explosives Co, E.C. and The New Explosives Co, Ltd.

SNELLING.   Ad; Ongar, Essex.
Kb; Nk.
Rm; The wording, SNELLING. ONGAR has been seen printed on some over-shot cards.

SOUTHERN COUNTIES AGRICULTURAL TRADING SOCIETY. (S.C.A.T.S.). [Id]. Ad; Salisbury, Wiltshire. (Rest of the Ad is Nk).
Kb; Un (12 Gg with 'Scatts' crest).

SOUTHERN COUNTIES AGRICULTURAL TRADING SOCIETY. (S.C.A.T.S.). [Id]. Ad; Winchester, Hampshire. (Rest of the Ad is Nk).
Kb; The Challenger Smokeless (12 Gg with cock pheasant on the tube).
Rm;The firms name was often abbreviated and pronounced as 'Scatts'. The Salisbury and Winchester branches are shown separately as they both sold different cartridges.

FREDERICK P. SPENCER. [Im]. Ad; 44 & 48 Lugley St, Newport, Isle of White.
Kb; F.P.S. Vectis Special Loading, Spencer's Vectis Bunnie, Spencer's Vectis Special.
Rm; He was shown as active in a 1907 trade directory. There was no trace of him in a 1911 directory.

GEORGE SPILLER. [Im]. Ad; Sherborne, Dorsetshire.
Kb; The Blackmoor Vale Special Cartridge.

SPORTING GUN & CARTRIDGE CO.   Ad; Derwent St, Derby, Derbys.
Kb; Nk.
Rm; They were know as active, Cr 1910.

SPORTING PARK.   Ad; 60 New Bond St, London W1.
Kb; Eley Ejector.
Rm; See, LONDON SPORTING PARK LTD in the Illustrated Section.

SPORTRIDGE (G.B.) LTD.   Ad; (Ad is Nk).
Kb; The Sportridge.

SPORTSMAN'S DEPOT.   Ad; Colchester, Essex. (Rest of the Ad is Nk).
Kb; Greased Lightning.

STACEY.   Ad; Dulverton, Somerset. (Rest of the Ad is Nk).
Kb; Nk.
Rm; Cartridge remains have been found with the stamping, STACEY No 12 DULVERTON.

PERCY STANBURY. [Gun and cartridge expert]. Ad; Mid Devon Cartridge Works, Exeter, Devonshire.
Kb; The Standby, Un.

STANGER.   Ad; Hull, Yorks (Humberside). (Rest of the Ad is Nk).
Kb; Nk.
Rm; Their name has been seen on an Eley Bros Ltd head-stamping.

STARMORE. [Im]. Ad; Sandford, Lincolnshire.
Kb; Un.

STENNER & CO.   Ad; Tiverton, Devonshire. (Rest of the Ad is Nk).
Kb & Rm; Their name has been seen on the head of a 12 Gg pinfire remains.

CHARLES W. STEPHENS.   Ad; Ledbury, Herefordshire (H & W).
Kb; Warranted Gas-tight Cartridge Case (Pinfire).

H. STEPHENS. [Im]. Ad; 35 West St, Horsham, Sussex.
Kb; Nk.
Rm; Cartridge remains have been found with Stephen's name on the stamping.

STEPHENSON.   Ad; Stokeseley, Yorkshire. (Rest of the Ad is Nk).
Kb; Nk.
Rm; Cartridge remains have been found by them.

MARK J. STEWART.   Ad; 114 South St, St Andrews, Fifeshire.
Kb; The Markmore, Special Smokeless Cartridge.

M. M. STEYTLER & CO.   Ad; Ad is Nk, may even be overseas.
Kb; Nk.
Rm; Cartridge remains have been found with a 12 Gg Eley stamping.

A. STOAKES.   Ad; Hastings, Sussex. (Rest of the Ad is Nk).
Kb; Nobel's Sporting Ballistite (Stoakes name on the over-shot card).

STOCKDALE.   Ad; Daybrook. ? (Location and Ad is Nk).
Kb; Un (Name on the over-shot card only).
Rm; The only reference that I have found to Daybrook is a road in London.

A. J. STOCKER & SON. Was also as, C. & E. STOCKER. [Im].
Ad; Fore St, Chulmleigh, Devonshire.
Kb; The Chulmleigh Cartridge, Stocker's Special Load.
Rm; A 1935 trade directory listed the firm as, Stocker A. J. There was no mention of a son.

F. E. STOCKER. [Im]. Ad; 5 Church St, St Austell, Cornwall.
Kb; Un (An Eley Bros Ltd case with Stocker's name on the stamping).

A. G. STOREY.   Ad; Ripon, North Yorks. (Rest of the Ad is Nk).
Kb; Dreadnought.

WILLIAM STOVIN. [Gm]. Ad; 4 Westgate, Grantham, Lincolnshire.
Kb; Un.
Rm; He was known to have been active, Cr 1892.

STOWIE.   Ad; Inverness, Inverness-shire (Highland). (Rest of Ad is Nk).
Kb; Nk.
Rm; A pinfire cartridge remains has been found with Stowie on the stamping.

ROBER STREET. [Im]. Ad; Long St, Tetbury, Gloucestershire.
Kb; Nk.
Rm; Cartridge remains have been found with his name on the stamping.

STUCHBERY'S STORES (THOMPSON P. & S. LTD). [Im, grocery and provisions]. Ad; 63, 65 & 67 High St, Maidenhead, Berkshire.
Kb; Un.
Rm; The only cartridge by them that I have seen was a dummy display round. They were listed in Kelly's directories for 1907 and 1920. They were not shown in the 1899 and 1903 directories.

STUDLEY.   Ad; Uffculme, Devonshire.
Kb; Un.
Rm; Their name was seen on an over-shot card that was loaded into a cartridge in the Tiverton Museum.

WILLIAM TARR. Later as, WILIAM TARR & SON. [Believed to have been hardware and Id merchants]. Ad; Minehead, Somerset. (Rest of Ad is Nk).
Kb; The Exmoor.
Rm; This business was once owned by, Palmer & Tarr. In 1913, J. Gliddon purchased the business from Tarr & Son and they continued to market the cartridge called, The Exmoor.

ELIJAH TARRANT.   Ad; 16 Sussex St, Cambridge, Cambridgeshire.
Kb; Nk.
Rm; Their cartridge remains have been found when metal detecting.

TAYLOR.   Ad; Wilmslow, Cheshire. (Rest of the Ad is Kn).
Kb & Rm; Over-shot cards printed, TAYLOR.WILMSLOW have been seen.

ALBERT VICTOR TAYLOR. [Gs, Gt]. Ad; 49 Bartholomew St, Newbury, Berkshire.
Kb; Mullerite Smokeless (Extra tube printings).
Rm; He was known to have been in business as a barber, Cr 1900. He started his Gs a few years later. He died in the late 1940's and his family continued to run the business until, Cr 1968.

C. H. TAYLOR & CO LTD. [Im]. Ad; 18 Market Place, Great Driffield, Yorks.
Kb; Un.

JOHN T. TAYLOR. Later as, J. T. TAYLOR & SON. [Im]. Ad; 90 High St, Bromsgrove, Worcestershire (Hereford & Worcester).
Kb; The Lightning Cartridge, Un.

TEMPLE & CO. [Im]. Ad; Church St, Basingstoke, Hampshire.
Kb; Nk.
Rm; Cartridge remains have been found. In an 1878 directory the firm was listed as, Temple & Portsmouth. By 1880 they were listed as, Temple & Co. They were not listed in a 1907 directory.

THACKER & CO. [Gt]. Ad; Worcester, Worcs (H & W). (Rest of Ad is Nk).
Kb; Eley Gastight Quality, Long Shot Smokeless.

E. W. R. THAIN.   Ad; Bramfield, Halesworth, Suffolk.
Kb; Un.

THOMPSON BROTHERS. [Im]. Ad; Bridgwater, Somerset.
Kb; New Special Smokeless, Ruby, The Special, Thompson's Special.

HERBERT THOMPSON. [Gm]. Ad; 22 West St, Boston, Lincolnshire.
Kb; Nk.

THORN & SON. [Possibly Im]. Ad; Heavitree, Exeter, Devonshire.
Kb; Nk.

THORNE BROTHERS. Also as, THORNE'S LTD.   Ad; Tiverton, Devon.
Kb; Smokeless Cartridge.
Rm; There has also been seen a Smokeless Cartridge by a William Thorne of Tiverton.

S. THORNLEY LTD. [Ammo dealers]. Ad; Snow Hill. Also at, 166 Deritend, Costa Green, Birmingham, Warwickshire (West Midlands).
Kb; Nk.

F. THRASHER.   Ad; 49 Coventry Rd, Birmingham, Warw (W. Midlands).
Kb; Un (Name on the over-shot card).

WILLIAM JAMES TICKNER. [Im]. Ad; High St, Bishop's Waltham, Hants.
Kb; The Sportsman.
Rm; William was known to have been active between, Cr 1898-1931.

G. S. TILBURY & F. A. JEFFRIES. [Mg]. Ad; Parson's Garage, Littlehampton Rd, Worthing, Sussex.
Kb; The Highdown.

WILLIAM C. TILL LTD. [Im]. Ad; 18 High St, Battle, Sussex.
Kb; Un.

TILY & BROWN LTD.   Ad; Guildford & Farnham, Surrey. Also at, Farnborough, Hampshire.
Kb; Farnford.

FREDERICK H. TIMS. [Gm]. Ad; 5 Cathedral Lane, Truro, Cornwall.
Kb; Un.
Rm; He was known to have been active, Cr 1902.

JOHN TINNING.   Ad; Longtown, Cumberland (Cumbria). Also at, Newcastleton, Roxburghshire.
Kb; Un.

P. TOVEY.   Ad; Midsomer Norton, Somerset (Avon).
Kb; Nk.

TOWY-TIVY-FARMERS. [Id]. Ad; Llanwrda, Carmarthenshire (Powys). Also at, Llansawel, Cardiganshire. And also at, Pumsaint, Lampeter, Cardiganshire (Dyfed).
Kb; Reward, The T.T. Super.

E. TOZER. Ad; Post Office Stores, Trevellas, Cornwall.
Kb; Un.

TREVOR & SONS. [Im]. Ad; 5 Elms Buildings, Seaside Rd, Eastbourne, Sussex.
Kb; Nk.
Rm; Kynoch 12 Gg head-stamping has been found by them.

S. TUDGE. [Gun shop]. Ad; Bewdley, Worcestershire (Hereford & Worcester).
Kb; Nk.
Rm; An over-shot card that was worded, S.TUDGE.BEWLEY was seen loaded into a cartridge by, N. W. Roberts & Co, of Rhyl.

W. TULLOCH & CO. [Gm]. Ad; 4 Bishopsgate Churchyard, New Broad St, London EC.
Kb; The Special.

TURNBULL. Ad; Bridgnorth, Shropshire. (Rest of the Ad is Nk).
Kb; Un.

J. TURNER. Ad; Penrith, Cumberland (Cumbria). (Rest of Ad is Nk).
Kb; Un.

J. A. TWYBLE. [Im]. Ad; Potadown, County Down, Northern Ireland.
Kb; The Invincible, Long Range, Surekiller.

LOHN UGLOW. [Gm, Gs,Gd and cycle agent]. Ad; Bullen St, Thorverton, Devonshire.
Kb; The Demon.
Rm; Judging by the list that he called himself, he must have had his fingers in several pies.

UNDERHILL. Ad; Newport. Also at, Eccleshall, Staffordshire.
Kb; Un (Pinfire).

UNITED KINGDOM CARTRIDGE CLUB (U.K.C.C.). [Collectors Club, U.K.).
Kb; First Anniversary Cartridge (The only crimp closed listed in this book).
Rm; The U.K.C.C. was founded at Boxford, Berks on the 6th of May 1990 by the amalgamation of the British Cartridge Collectors Club (B.C.C.C.) and KRUCKL. Those letters stood for Ken Rutterford's United Kigndom Cartridge List and pronounced as 'Cruckle'. Having founded KRUKCL and being a founder member of the U.K.C.C. I feel that I have the artistic licence to include this club and it's cartridge within this list, even though it was crimp closed.

UTTING & BUCKENHAM. [Gd, Im]. Ad; East Dereham, Norfolk.
Kb; Nk.

WILLIAM VARLEY. [Gm]. Ad; 3 Midland St, Hull, Yorkshire (Humberside).
Kb; Un.

VAUGHAN.   Ad; 39 The Strand, London.
Kb; Nk.
Rm; A 12 Gg head-stamping has been found by them.

J. C. VAUX.   Ad; Hanwell, Ealing, London.
Kb; Un (Their name was on the over-shot card only).

SAMUEL VEALS & Son. [Gm]. Ad; 3 Tower Hill, Bristol, Glos (Avon).
Kb; Nk.
Rm; A 12 Gg head-stamping has been found. They were known to have been active, Cr 1906-1910.

VERSY.   Ad; Bristol, Gloucestershire (Avon). (Rest of the Ad is Nk).
Kb; Nk.
Rm; I was once told of a 16 Gg grey coloured cartridge by them.

F. VICKERY.   Ad; Luxborough, Somerset. (Rest of the Ad is Nk).
Kb; Nk.
Rm; The name was seen printed on an over-shot card.

VINCENT BROTHERS.   Ad; Ottery St Mary, Devonshire.
Kb; The Invincible Cartridge.

W. A. & A. T. CO.   Ad; London. ? (Rest of the Ad is Nk).
Kb; Nk.
Rm; This listed firm was printed on an over-shot card that was loaded into a,
F. Joyce & Co Ltd pinfire cartridge.

J. H. WADDON.   Ad; Wedmore, Somerset.
Kb; Special Smokeless Cartridge.

JOHN WADDON & SONS. [Im]. Ad; Bridgnorth, Shropshire.
Kb; Un.

JOHN WADDON & SONS.   Ad; Bridgwater, Somerset.
Kb; The Quantock.
Rm; Over the years I have gleaned information from many people. I have had to take them at their word. Now having two John Waddon & Sons with one at Bridgnorth and the othe at Bridgwater may just be a coincidence. Yet on the other hand, one of them might be a mistake.

WAGER & SONS.   Ad; Honiton, Devonshire. (Rest of the Ad is Nk).
Kb; Nk.
Rm; Their name has been seen printed on an over-shot card.

WAKEFIELD.   Ad; Taunton, Somerset. (Rest of the Ad is Nk).
Kb; Nk.
Rm; A headstamping has been found in cartridge remains in 12 Gg with the wording, Wakefield Taunton.

A. E. & A. WALKER. [Im]. Ad; Tenbury Wells, Worcestershire (H & W).
Kb; Un.

JAMES B. WALKER. [Gd]. Ad; 63 Newgate St, Newcastle –upon-Tyne, Nthb.
Kb; The Newgate.

R. WALKER.   Ad; (Ad is Nk).
Kb; Nk.
Rm; Held patents for metal over-shot wads. It is quite possible that he might have placed his name on some of them.

WALKER & COOKE.   Ad; Bromyard, Herefordshire (H & W).
Kb; Nk.

H. WALKINGTON. [Gd]. Ad; Bridlington, Yorkshire (Humberside).
Kb; The Reliable.

WILLIAM WALLAS. [Gm]. Ad; 66 King St, Wigton, Cumberland (Cumbria).
Kb ;Eley Pegamoid, Un.

WALLIS BROTHERS. [Gm, cycle agents, locksmiths, Bell hangers, fitters and Electrical engineers]. Ad; 156 & 364 High St. Also, 4 St Mary's St. And also, 4 Corporation St & 1 Cornhill, Lincoln, Lincs. Also at 20 Norfolk St, Sunderland, County Durham (Tyne & Wear).
Kb; The Big Tom of Lincoln, Gastight Cartridge Case, Smokeless Cartridge, Walbro Special.
Rm; They started trading in Lincoln, Cr 1885 at 364 High St. It was known that one of the brothers had a Gs business in Spalding. By 1892 the firm was at 156 High St. By 1937 the firms Ad was at, 4 St Mary's St. It was in 1939 that Wallis Bros joined forces with Skemptons. See the next entry in this list.

WALLIS BROTHERS & SKEMPTONS. (For trades and Ad, se the last entry).
Kb; The Big Tom of Lincoln, The Lincoln Imp.
Rm; The Big Tom of Lincoln took its name from a large bell in the tower of Lincoln Cathedral. This firm stopped trading , Cr 1959.

WARD & TAYLOR. [Im]. Ad; Leominster, Herefordshire (H & W).
Kb; Un.

WARNERS. [General stores]. Ad; Barrack St, Bantry, County Cork, Republic of Ireland.
Kb; Un.

A. E. WARREN. [Gm]. Ad; 116 Peascot St, Windsor, Berkshire.
Kb; The Windsor Special.
Rm; An old head-stamping has been found,
B.WARREN No 12 WINDSOR/ KYNOCH.

GEORGE ANTHONY WARREN. [Im]. Ad; 7 North St, Horncaslte. Also at, Spilsby, Lincolnshire.
Kb; The Warren.

JAMES WATSON & SON. [Gm]. Ad; 24 Guild St, Aberdeen, Aberdeenshire (Grampian).
Kb; The Dead Shot.
Rm; James was a successor to William Calder of the same Ad.

ROWLAND WATSON. [Cl, Gm]. Ad; Victoria Gun Works, 19 Whittal St, Birmingham, Warwickshire (West Midlands).
Kb; Eley Blue Case, Eley Brown Case, Joyce Red Case, Royal Green Case, Royal Red Case.
Rm; He had his works at the Rose & Crown Yard, Whittal St. This may have been his Victoria Gun Works. He was known to have been active, Cr 1897-1908.

WATSON BRACEWELL. [Mullerite agent]. Ad; Peebles, Peebles-shire (Borders).
Kb; Mullerite Yellow Seal (Extra tube printings).

WEBB.   Ad; Hull, Yorks (Humberside). (Rest of the Ad is Nk).
Kb; Nk.
Rm; Cartridge remains have been found with the stamping, WEBB.HULL. ELEY 12 LONDON.

WEBBER & SAUNDERS. [Im]. Ad; Tiverton, Devonshire.
Kb;The Pheasant, Sure Shot.

WEBLEY & SCOTT LTD. Also as, WEBLEY & SCOTT REVOLVER & ARMS CO LTD. [Gm]. Ad; 81-91 Weaman St, Birmingham, Warw (W. Midlands). Also at; 7 Shaftsbury Avenue London W.
Kb; Nk.
Rm; It is just possible that they may have had their name on a cartridge.

WEBSTERS. [Im]. Ad; Axminster, Devonshire.
Kb; The Axe Valley.

W. R. WEDGWOOD. (See MORROW & CO, in the Illustrated Section).

C. WEEKES & CO. [Gs]. Ad; Dublin, Republic of Ireland. (Rest of Ad is Nk).
Kb; Weekes Patent (Brass 8Gg).

F. WEEKS.   Ad; Lymington, Hampshire. (Rest of the Ad is Nk).
Kb; Un.

W. A. WELCH. [Sm and pathletic outfitter]. Ad; 90-92 Southampton Rd, Also at, 2E High St, Eastleigh, Hampshire.
Kb; The Pheasant Cartridge.
Rm; It is not known for sure if W.A. Welch had his name printed on the cartridges, but he did have it stamped on the boxes that contained Pheasant Cartridges from Patstone & Cox of Southampton.

EDWARD WEST.   Ad; Tetbury, Gloucestershire. (Rest of Ad is Nk).
Kb; Nk.
Rm; I was told that Ted West once sold cartridges that carried his name.

WESTGATE ESTATE. [Possibly a private country estate]. (Ad is Nk).
Kb; Westgate Estate.

WESTLEY RICHARDS & CO LTD. [Gm]. Ad; 12 Corporation St. Later at, 24 Bennett's Hill, Birmingham, Warw (W.Midlands). Also at, New Bond St. Later at, 23 Conduit St, London W1.
Kb; The A.L.P. Cartridge, The Aquatite, The Carlton, The Explora (Hollow slug load), The Fauneta (Ball loaded), Pegamoid, The Regent (Ejector metal covered), The Right & Left, The Special, Super Magnum Explora, Westley Richards Special Accelerated L.P. Loading, The Wizard.
Rm; This firm moved from Corporation St, to Conduit St, in September 1917. From there they ran their own shooting school from grounds at West Hendon. A special version of their Wizard Cartridge was sold at the school.

J. WESTON.   Ad; Northwich, Cheshire.
Kb; Kynoch Nitrone (Weston's name on the over-shot card only).

JOSEPH WHEATER. [Gm]. Ad; 7 Queen St. Also at, 27-29 Anlaby Rd, Hull, Yorkshire (Humberside).
Kb; The Humber.
Rm; Joe took over the business of R. Robinson who had also marketed a Humber Cartridge.

WHITE.   Ad; Northampton, Northants. Also in, Paris, France.
Kb; Nk.
Rm; Cartridge remains were found with the stamping,
WHITE. NORTHAMPTON & PARIS No12.

J. P. WHITLOCK. Later as, J. P. WHITLOCK & SONS. [Im].
Ad; 18 Market Square, Holsworthy, Devonshire.
Kb; The Whitlock.

WHOLESALE ARMS & AMMUNITION TRADING CO. [Gd].
Ad; 40 St Andrew's, Queen Victoria St, London EC.
Kb; Un.

WIGGLESWORTH.   Ad; Thirsk, Yorkshire. (Rest of the Ad is Nk)..
Kb; Nk.
Rm; Cartridge remains with Wigglesworth on the stamping has been found.

THOMAS J. WILD & CO. [Gm]. Gun Works, 10 & 19 Whittal St, Birmingham, Warwickshire (West Midlands).
Kb; Special Red Cartridge, Un.
Rm; See R. Watson in this list as he also used this same Ad.

WILDER.   Ad; Birmingham, Warw (W. Midlands). (Rest of Ad is Nk).
Kb; Parachute Cartridge (A very long and large cartridge).

WILKINSON. [Im]. Ad; Durham, County Durham. (Rest of Ad is Kn).
Kb; Un.

JAMES WILKINSON & SON. Also as, WILKINSON SWORD CO LTD. [Gm and sword, etc]. Ad; 27 Pall Mall. Also at, Southfield Rd, Acton, London W.
Kb; Ejector, Pinfire (15 Gg), Regal, Special, Wilkinson Waterproof.

JOSEPH WILLIAM WILLCOCKS. [Im]. Ad; 14 St Mary's St. Also at, 2 Ironmonger St, Stamford, Lincolnshire.
Kb; Eley's Gas-tight Cartridge Case for E.C. Gunpowder.

C. D. WILLIAMS.   Ad; 86 Ann St. Later at, 71-73 Victoria St, Belfast, Northern Ireland.
Kb; Kynoch Patent Perfectly Gas-tight (Williams name on the head-stamping).

E. WILLIAMS. [Gs]. Ad; Aberystwyth, Cardiganshire (Dyfed).
Kb; The Regent.

HARRY WILLIAMS. [Im]. Ad; 49 Pyle St, Newport, Isle of Wight.
Kb; The Express, Un.

J. S. WILLIAMS. [Im and explosives merchant]. Ad; Pontypridd, Glamorgan.
Kb; Un.

T. M. WILLIAMS. [Im]. Ad; Llandilo, Carmarthenshire (Dyfed).
Kb; The Rabbit.

CHARLES WILLIAM WILLIAMSON. [Gm]. Ad; 3 Bridge Rd, Stockton-on-Tees, County Durham (Cleveland).
Kb; Un.

DUDLEY WILLIAMSON. [Gs]. 3 George St, Kettering, Northamptonshire.
Kb; Special Smokeless Cartridge.

EDWIN WILSON. [Gm, pistol and rifle]. Ad; 13 Rampant Horse St, Norwich, Norfolk.
Kb; Un.

GEOFFREY WILSON. [Gm]. Ad; 15 Belmont Bridge, Skipton, Yorkshire.
Kb; Wilkill Smokeless Cartridge.

GEOFFREY H. WILSON. [Gm]. Ad; 9 Market Place, Horncastle, Lincolnshire.
Kb; The Champion.
Rm; Arthur Hill took over this firm at the same Ad in 1902.

THEO WILSON & SONS LTD. [Im]. Ad; Clitheroe, Lancs. (Rest of Ad is Nk).
Kb; Champion Smokeless.

WILTON & NICHOLLS. [Im]. Ad; 18 Market Jew St, Penzance, Cornwall.
Kb; The Riviera.

L. J. WINSLADE LTD.   Ad; 4 Central Buildings, Bath Place, Worthing, Sussex.
Kb; Nk.

WILLIAM WITCHELL. [Im]. Ad; Church St, Tetbury, Gloucestershire.
Kb; Nk.

WOOD.   Ad; Bristol, Gloucestershire (Avon). Also at, Cardiff, Glamorgan.
Kb; Nk.
Rm; A cartridge has been seen with the name 'Wood' on the over-shot card. It was loaded into a Joyce case that had a Bailey's Patent Gas-check. The case wall printings include, 'Patent Machinery'.

F. WOOD.   Ad; Salisbury, Wiltshire. (Rest of the Ad is Nk).
Kb; Un (Pinfire).

GEORGE WOOD & CO. [Gs]. Ad; Sheffield, Yorkshire. (Rest of the Ad is Nk).
Kb; Nk.
Rm; This firm was absorbed into, H. B. Suggs of Nottingham.

J. L. WOOD. [Gm]. Ad; St Mary's St, Stamford, Lincolnshire.
Kb; Un.

WOOD & HORSPOOL. [Im]. 114 Pyle St, Newport, Isle of Wight.
Kb; Un (Seen in both pin and centre fire).
Rm; Cr 1880, there was, W. F. Wood at 41 High St. Cr 1907, Arthur Wood was active at 114 Pyle St. In 1911, Wood & Horspool were listed as being at 114 Pyle St. Come 1915, Arthur was shown as being at 114 Pyle St. From then on the shop was in the name of Arthur up until Cr 1960's. The partnership with Horspool could not have lasted long. See ARTHUR WOOD (NEWPOT I.W.) in the Illustrated Section.

T. P. WOOD & CO.   Ad; Bristol, Glos (Avon). Also at, Cardiff, Glamorgan.
Kb; Nk.
Rm; Remains by them has been found by metal detecting.

WOOD PAGE & CO.   Ad; 39-40 Walcot St, Bath, Somerset (Avon).
Kb; Un.
Rm; See PAGE WOOD & Co, in the Illustrated Section.

WOODISSE & DESBOROUGH. [Im]. Ad; Market Place, Ashbourne, Debys.
Kb; The Premier.
Rm; This firm was listed in a 1932 directory as, Woodisse & Co.

WOODROW & CO LTD. [Cl, Im]. Ad; Castle St, Salisbury, Wiltshire.
Kb; Nk
Rm; I was told that cartridges were once loaded on their premises.

JAMES WRIGHT. [Im]. Ad; Oakhampton, Devonshire. (Rest of Ad is Nk).
Kb; Special Load.

JOHN WRIGHT. [Im]. Ad; 1 Churchgate, Spalding, Lincolnshire.
Kb; Amberite Cartridge..

WRIGHT & CURREY.   Ad; Spalding, Lincolnshire. (Rest of the Ad is Nk).
Kb; Amberite Cartridge.
Rm; At one time there was an Im named, John Wright who traded from,
1 Churchgate, Spalding, who also sold an Amberite. This makes me think that
there must have been family connections with this firm and those of John
Wright and that of, Randall Wright.

WRIGHTS.   Ad; Maldon. Also at, Southend-on-Sea, Essex.
Kb; What Ho!!! Smokeless.

S. YOUNG & SONS.   Ad; Misterton, Somerset.
Kb; Frank Dyke's Yellow Wizard (Extra tube printings).
Rm; See FRANK DYKE & CO LTD in the Illustrated Section.

END OF THE FIRMS CARTRIDGE LIST.

UNIDENTIFIED CARTRIDGES

These are cartridges that did not carry their makers names, but they did carry a brand name of such. There have been times when a box of cartridges has been purchased with their brand names printed on the cartridge box. Only once opened the cartridges that the box contained were found to have no printings on their case walls. This kind of thing was common during the two world wars as economy was the order of those difficult times.

Listed below are just a few of the many unidentified cartridges that have surfaced in the British Isles. These I have taken to have been from these isles, but of this I cannot be certain. There is also that possibility that some of these may have been produced for marketing in the British Empire. Later to be called, the British Commonwealth. There are so many questions that one would like to know of their answers. Unfortunately, those people that had those answers are now long gone.

Those that are listed below that are followed by an asterisk so *, can be seen in the last pages of the Illustrated Section.

UNIDENTIFIED

20 Gauge 20. Smokeless Gastight.
The Black Thistle Special Smokeless.
C A B. *
Crown Brand C C B. *
The Country Club. *
Gastight Metal Lined.
Ideal London. *
LODA. *
M. & C. CA. (On the head-stamping).
Metalode Metal Lined Cartridge.
The Rabbit Special.
Smokeless Cartridge.
Smokeless Metal Lined Cartridge.
Special British.
Speedway. *
The Supreme.
Tiger Brand.
The Trojan. *
The Union Jack Brand Cartridge. *
The Windsor Cartridge.

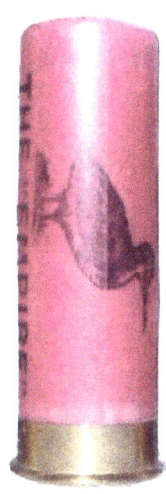   

SECTION TWO
The Illustrations with written listings

  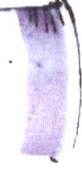 

HENRY ADKIN. [Gm]. Ad; 57 High St. Also at, Castle Rd, Bedford, Beds.
Kb; 20 Gauge, Ajax, Demon, Reliance, Special Loading.

J. AGNEW.   Ad; 118 High St, Colchester, Essex.
Kb; Special Smokeless Gastight.

HENRY ESAU AKRILL. [Gm]. Ad; 18 Market Place, Beverley,
Yorks (Humberside).
Kb; The Collector, The County, The Holderness, Pegamoid,
The Special Cartridge, The Universal.

 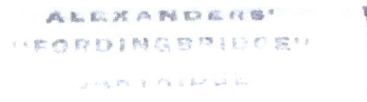 

ALEXANDER BROS. [Im and general stores]. Ad; High St,
Fordingbridge, Hants.
Kb; The Fordingbridge (shown above).

  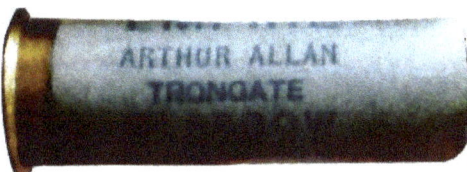

ARTHUR ALLAN LTD. [Gm]. Ad; 144 Trongate. Later at, 3 West Nile St, Glasgow, Lanarks (Strathclyde).
Kb; Empire, Famous A.A., The Imperial, Super A.A., Three Star.
Rm; Established 1863. Ceased trading from Trongate in 1925.

ALTHAM & SON. Ad; Penrith, Cumberland (Cumbria).
Kb; Eley's Pegamoid, Sure Kill.

JOHN ANDERSON & SO. [Cl,Gm, Gd].
Ad; 52 Market Place, Maldon, Yorks.
Kb; The Derwent Cartridge (Shown above),
The Eclipse, The Malton 410, The Rabbit.

 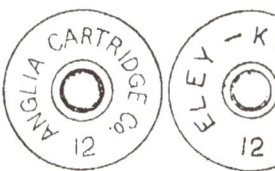

ANGLIA CARTRIDGE CO. [Am]. Ad; Taverham, Norwich, Norfolk.
Kb; Anglia (shown above).
Rm; There were other brands such as , Red Rival, but as these were six fold crimp closed they are not included in this book.

 ARMSTRONGS (SPORTING GUN DEPOT). Also as, ARMSTRONG & CO. [Field Sports]. Ad; 10 Neville St, Newcastle-upon-Tyne, Northumberland (Tyne & Wear). Kb; The A.C.C., The C Cartridge (shown above), Gastight, Pressure Reducing Case, Recoil Reducing.

ARMY & NAVY CO-OPERATIVE SOCIETY LTD. Later changed to, ARMY & NAVY STORES LTD. [Ds, Gm]. Ad; 8 Howick Place, Westminster. Also at, 105 Victoria St, Westminster, London SW1.
Kb; The Coronation Cartridge, The Every Day Cartridge, The Every Day Nitro, Pegamoid, The Reliable, The Victoria.
Rm; They had overseas branches in Bombay, Calcutta and Karach. One of these overseas brands was, The Services Cartridge.

S. R. ARNOLD. [Gs]. Ad; Louth, Lincs.
Kb; Express Special.

HENRY ATKIN LTD. [Gm]. Ad; 18 Oxendon St West. Was also at, 2 Jermyn St. Later at, 88 Jermyn St. Later still, 27 St James's St, London SW.
Kb; The Covert, Ejector, The Ever Ready, The Gem, The Jermyn, Pegamoid, The Raleigh. Rm; Joined Grant & Lang and became Atkin Grant & Lang.

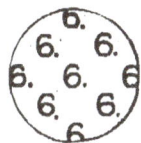 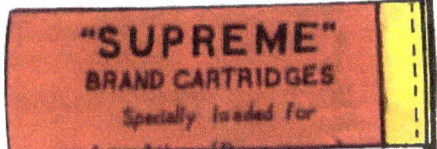 

JOHN ATKINS (DUNMANWAY) LTD.
Ad; Dunmanway, County Cork, Republic of Ireland.
Kb; Supreme (drawing shown above).

WILLIAM ATKINSON. Later as, W. ATKINSON & SONS. [Gm and fishing tackle]. Ad; 20 Market St and North Rd, Lancaster. Also at, 11 Skipton St, Morecambe, Lancs. Also at Kendal, Westmorland (Cumbria).
Kb; Eley Grand Prix Case, Lancaster Castle Brand (Paradox slug or shot), Utility Smokeless. Rm; Known active at 20 Market St circa 1886-87.

ATKINSON & GRIFFIN. [Gm or Gs]. Ad; 58 Highgate, Kendal, Westmorland (Cumbria).
Kb; Reliable.

T. C. AUSTIN. [Gm]. Ad; 16 Welselry Rd, Ashford, Kent.
Kb; Eley Case.
Rm; Several have been seen with Austin's name on the tubes.

AVERILL & SON.   Ad; Evesham, Worcs (Hereford & Worcester).
Kb; Averill's Express (shown above).

BACON & CURTIS LTD. [Im wholsale and retail]. Ad; 44 & 180 High St, Poole, Dorset. Also at, 106 Christchurch Rd, Bournemouth, Hants (Dorset).
Kb; Un (Their name on the over shot card only).
Rm; Known to have been active between 1907 and 1939 and maybe longer.

BAGNALL & KIRKWOOD. [Gm and fishing tackle]. Ad; 31 Westgate Rd, Newcastle-upon-Tyne, Northumberland (Tyne & Wear).
Kb; The Pointer, The Setter (shown above), The Tyne.

 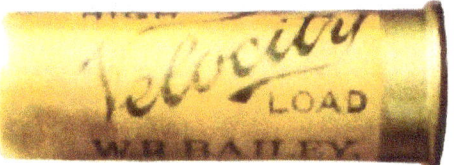 

W. R. BAILEY. [Im and agricultural dealer]. Ad; Congresbury, Som.
Kb; High Velocity Load, The Somerset Velocity.

JOSEPH BAKER & SON. [Im, Gm]. Ad; Market Place. Also at, Norwich St, Fakenham, Norfolk.
Kb; Baker's Special, Union Jack, West Norfolk.

J. T. BAKER. [Gun and fishing tackle dealer]. Ad; 103 Victoria Rd, Darlington, County Durham.
Kb; Sipe Smokeless (Italian L. E. Personne cartridge).

W. E. BAKER. Later as, W. E. BAKER & CO. [Im]. Ad; 2 Bedford Square. Also at, North St, Tavistock, Devon.
Kb; Un (shown above).

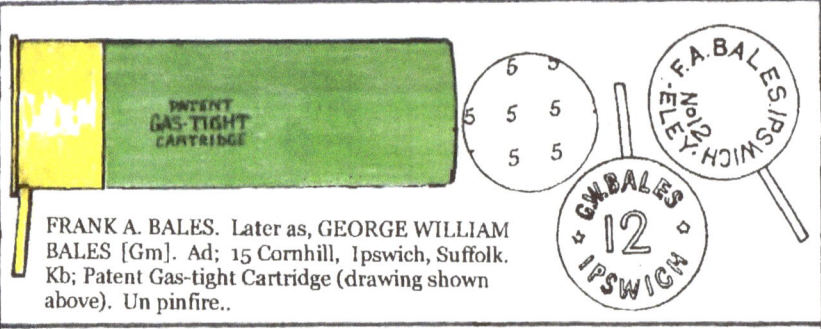

FRANK A. BALES. Later as, GEORGE WILLIAM BALES [Gm]. Ad; 15 Cornhill, Ipswich, Suffolk. Kb; Patent Gas-tight Cartridge (drawing shown above). Un pinfire..

BAPTY & CO LTD. [Arms retailers]. Ad; 703 Harrow Rd, London E11. Kb; Un (Bapty's name on over shot card, drawing shown above).

 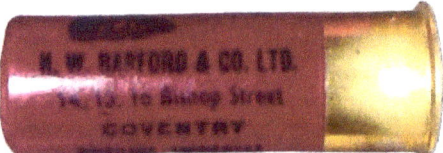 

H. W. BARFORD & CO LTD.   Ad; 14-16 Bishop St, Coventry, Warw (West Midlands).
Kb; Special Imperial.

HENRY BARHAM. Later as, C.H. BARHAM. [Gm]. Ad; Sun St. Also at, 95 Tilehouse St, Hitchin, Herts.
Kb; The Challenge, The Comet Cartridge, The Hert's Cartridge (shown above).

BARKERS. Ad; Corner House, Huddersfield, Yorks.
Kb; De Luxe (shown above).

BARNARD & LEVERT. [Im]. Ad; Bird St, Lichfield, Staffs.
Kb; Un.

ALBERT A. BARNES. [Gm]. Ad; Market Place, Ulverston, Lancs (Cumbria).
Kb; The Lonsdale, The Referendum.

GEORGE JAS BARNES. Later became, G. J. BARNES & SONS. [Im].
Ad; 29 Church St, Calne, Wilts.
Kb; Kynoch's Perfectly Gas-tight Cartridge (Barne's name only on the stamping, drawing shown above).
Rm; Directories have shown George in 1920 and with sons in 1927.

 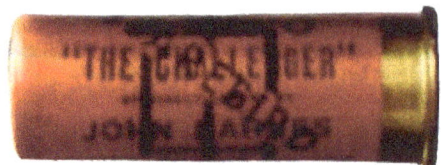 

JOHN BARNES. [Gm]. Ad; Burn's Statue Square, Ayr, Ayrs.
Kb; The Challenger, The Chieftain.

WILLIAM BARNES. [Im]. Ad; Market Place, Ashbourne, Derbys.
Kb; Special Red, Un.

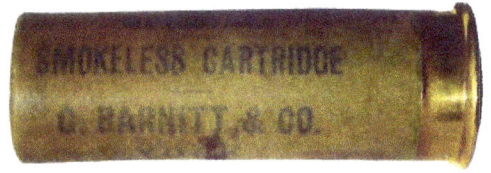 

G. BARNITT & CO.   Ad; Colliergate, York, Yorks.
Kb; Barnitt's Special, Special Smokeless Cartridge (shown above).

GEORGE THORPE BARTRAM. [Gm]. Ad; 35 & 44 Bank St, Braintree, Essex.
Kb; Bartram's Hard Hitters (shown above), High Velocity.

GEORGE JAS BASSETT. [Im]. Ad; 4Swan St, Petersfield, Hants.
Kb; The Champion.
Rm; This firm was founded in 1927.

GEORGE BATE (GUNMAKERS) LTD. [Gm]. Ad; 132 Steelhouse Lane, Birmingham, Warw (W. Midlands).
Kb; The Game, The Im perial, The Leader.
Rm; This firm was known at the above address as early as 1908.

GEORGE BATES [Gs]. Ad; 126 Seaside Rd, Eastbourne, Sussex.
Kb; The Eastbourne, The Mallard Gastight, The Reliable.

EDWARD BAYS & CO. [Im and general furnishing].
Ad; 22 Wood St, Swindon (Old Town). Also at, Faringdon St, Swindon, Wilts..
Kb; Un (drawing shown above).
Rm; He was known to have been active as early as 1903.

BARKER BROS.   Ad; Grantham, Lincs.
Kb; Mullerite Smokeless (Barker's name on the tube).

H. & S. BEARE. [Im]. Ad; 80 Queen St, Newton Abbot, Devon.
Kb; The Sharpshooter, Smokeless Sharpshooters.

 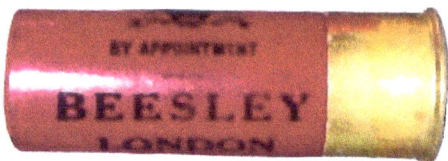 

FREDERICK BEESLEY. [Gm]. Ad; 2 St James's St, London SW.
Kb; Kynock's Grouse Ejector, Un (shown above).

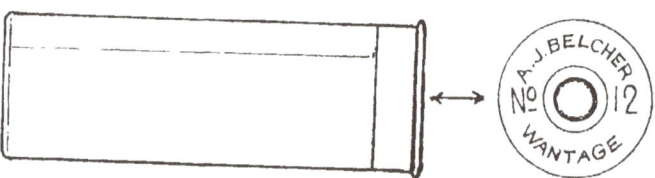

A.J. BELCHER. [Im]. Ad; Market Place. Also at, Newbury St, Wantage, Berks (Oxon).
Rm; No known cartridge exists. Provisional drawing from cartridge remains. Not shown in 1887 directory, but shown in directories for 1895 and onwards.

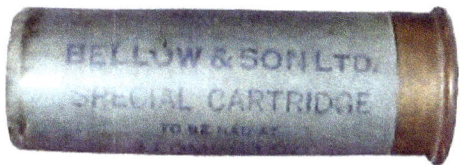

BELLOW & SON.   Ad; Leominster, Hereford & Bromyard, Herfs (H & W).
Als o at Tenbury Wells, Worcs (Hereford & Worcester).
Kb;Special Cartridge (shown above).

BENHAM ESTATE. (SUTTON'S SETTELED ESTATES). {Es}.
Ad; Estate Office, Bradford's Farm, Marsh Benham, Newbury,Berks.
Kb; Un (shown above). Rm; Most likely printed by this private estate.

A. BENIGNO. [Retailer in guns and ammunition].
Ad; 12-14 High St, Peebles, Peebles-shire (Borders).
Kb; Un (drawing shown above).

JOSEPH BENTLEY. [Cl]. Ad; 309 Halifax Rd, Liversedge, Yorks.
Kb; The Croft (shown above).
Rm; joe used Greenbat powder and loaded into Greenwood & Batley cases.
Closures were either rolled turn-over or six fold crimp.

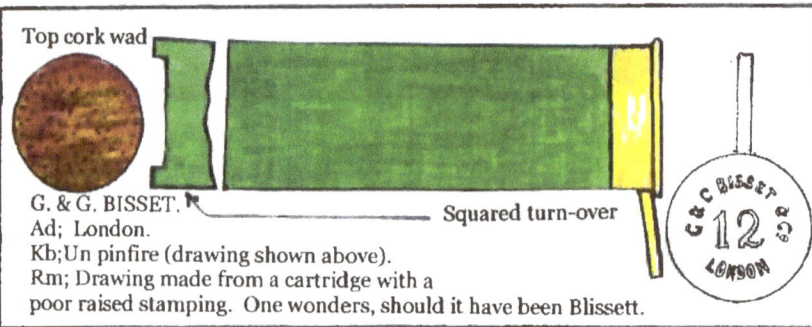

Top cork wad

G. & G. BISSET.
Ad; London.
Kb;Un pinfire (drawing shown above).
Rm; Drawing made from a cartridge with a poor raised stamping. One wonders, should it have been Blissett.

Squared turn-over

J. BLACK. [Gun dealer]. Ad; Bollington, Near Macclesfield, Ches.
Kb; The Bollin (shown above).

  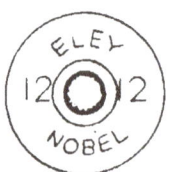

JAMES BLAKE. [Dealer in guns]. Ad; 12 The Square, Kelso, Roxburghs (Borders).
Kb; The Roxburgh, Roxburgh Special Smokeless.

JOHN BLANCH & SON. [Gm pistol and rifle]. Ad; 29 Gracechurch St.
Also at, 4 Bishopgate Churchyard, London EC2.
Kb; Ejector, Kynoch's Grouse Ejector, Improved Gas-tight Cartridge, Un.
Rm; They were incorporated in to the business of Alfred Davis.

RICHARD BLANTON. [Gm], Ad; Market Place, Ringwood, Hants.
Kb; The Competitor, The Imperial.

THOMAS BLAND & SONS. [Gm]. Ad; 430 West Strand. Later at,
King William St, London EC4.
Kb; The 'B', The Bee, Pegamoid, Un.

 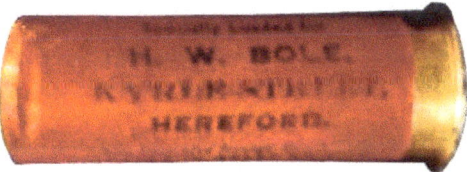 

H. W. BOLE.   Ad; Kyrle St, Hereford, Herefs (H & W).
Kb; The Kyrle Cartridge.

GEORGE EDWARD BOND & SON. [Gm, Cl]. Ad;; 2 Castle St, Thetford, Norfolk.
Kb; The Bond, Eley's Ejector, Gastight 410, The Invincible.
Rm; Were known active between 1904 and 1916 and perhaps for longer.

  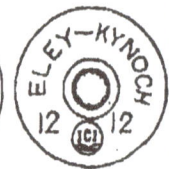

BOSS & CO LTD. [Gm, Cl]. Ad; 13 Dover St. Later at, 41 Albemarle St. Then at, 13-14 Cork St, London W1.
Kb; Brown Brand, Ejector, Green Brand, High Velocity, Orange Brand, Pegamoid, Regent, Special, Special High Velocity, Un.

CHARLES BOSWELL. [Gm and rifle]. Ad; 126 The Strand.
Later at, 15 Mill St, Hanover Square, London W1.
Kb; Kynoch's Grouse Ejector, Special Express (shown above), Un.

 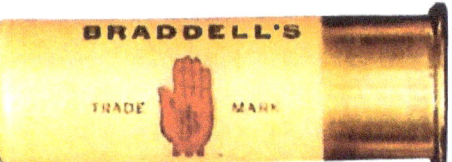 

JOSEPH BRADELL & SON LTD. [Gm]. Ad; Mayfair, Arthur Square, Belfast 1, Northern Ireland.
Kb; The Castle, De Luxe Special, Ejector, Eley Ejector, The Empire, The J.B., The Meteor, The Mors, The Special, Special Gastight, The Victory, Un, including pinfires.   Rm; Established in 1811.

WILLIAM BRITT & SONS. [Im].
Ad; 21 South St, Chesterfield, Derbys.
Kb; The Sydenham Cartridge.
Rm; Sydenham named after a large glass dome. Known active as early as 1881. It closed its doors in the mid 1980's.

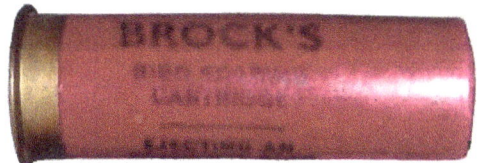

BROCK'S EXPLOSIVES. [Pyrotechnic manufacturers]. Ad; Hemel Hempstead, Herts.
Kb; Bird Scaring Cartridge (Ejects a humming star).

BROOKER.   Ad; Hitchin, Herts.
Kb; Un.

F. BUCK.   Ad; Wincanton, Somerset.
Kb; Eley Gastight Quality Case (Buck's name on top card only).

J. BUCKLAND. Later as, J. BUCKLAND & SONS.   Ad; Taunton, Som.
Kb; Taunton Special Smokeless (shown above).

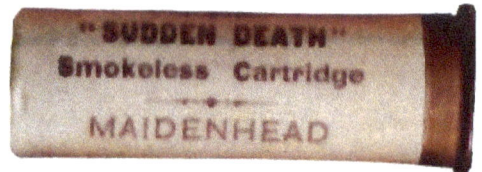 

JOHN BUDGEN & CO. [Im]. Ad; 49 & 51 High St, Maidenhead, Berks.
Kb; Sudden Death Smokeless

A. C. BULPIN.   Ad; Newton Abbot, Devon.
Kb; Bulpin's Straight Shot Cartridge.

W. BUNTING.   Ad; Cromford, Near Wirksworth, Derbys.
Kb; Mullerite Green Seal, Mullerite Grey Seal (shown above), Mullerite Yellow Seal.
Rm; Mullerite cartridges were with extra tube printings.

 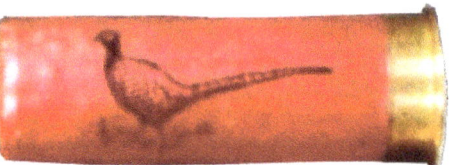 

FREDERICK H. BURGESS LTD.   Ad; Eccleshall, , Near Newcastle-Under-Lyme. Also at, Wolverhampton, Staffs. And also at, Newport & Shrewsbury, Salop.
Kb; Champion.

JAMES BURROW. [Gm or Gs]. Ad; 116 Fishergate, Preston, Lancs.
Also at, 46 Lowther St, Carlisle, Cumberland (Cumbria).
Kb; The Economic, The Challenge, Eley's Gastight Case (extra tube printings),
Eley Gas-tight Cartridge Case (Burrow's name only on the over shot card),
The Field, Kynoch's Grouse Ejector, The Paragon.

 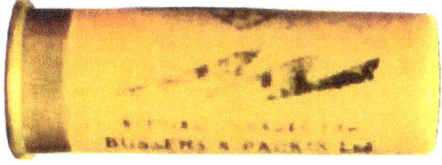 

BUSSEMS & PARKIN LTD. [Im]. Ad; Mildenhall, Suffolk.
Kb; Un.

GEORGE G. BUSSEY & CO.   Ad; London (Rest of Ad is not known).
Kb; Full brass ejector (Bussey's name on the stamping (shown above), Pinfire Un.

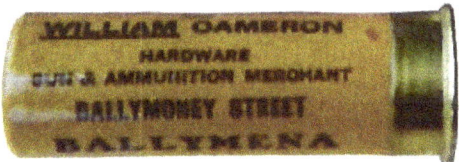

WILLIAM CAMERON. Later as, W. CAMERON & CO. [Gun and ammo dealers].
Ad; Ballymena, County Antrim, Northern Ireland.
Kb; The Cameronia, Cameron's Special.

R. CAMPBELL & SONS.   Ad; Leyburn, Yorks.
Kb; The Special Cartridge, The Wensledale.

 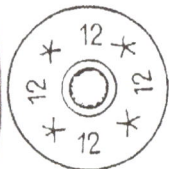

CALEDONIAN CARTRIDGE CO. [Am]. Ad; Arrat Works, Brechin, Angus.
Kb; Un.
Rm; A late firm. Paper and plastic tubes. Rolled turn- over's and crimpings.

CAMBRIDGE & CO. [Im and gun dealers]. Ad; Carrickfergus, Northern Ireland.
Kb; The Antrim, The County Down, The Ulster (shown above).

RICHARD LOVAT CAPELL. [Im]. Ad; 47 Gold St. Also at, The Cattle Market, Northampton, Northants.
Kb; The Capella (shown above. Capell's name on the stamping).
Rm; Known to have been active between 1894 and 1924.

EARL OF CARNARVON. [Pc]. Ad; Highclere Castle, Highclere Estate, Highclere, Hants.
Kb; Un (drawing shown above, crest on over-shot card only).
Rm; Loaded for him by C. Hellis & Sons Ltd. Some had purple tubes with silver printing. The top card was white with dark blue printing.

CARR BROS. [Gm]. Ad; 3A Market St. Also at, Cloth Hall St, Huddersfield, Yorks.
Kb; Eley Ejector (Carr Bros on the stamping).

 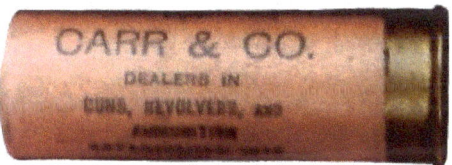 

E. P. CARR & CO. [Im, dealers in guns and ammunition].
Ad; 4 Lower Parliament St, Nottingham, Notts.
Kb; Ejector, Un.
Rm; Established in 1828. Was known active in 1912 and perhaps later.

 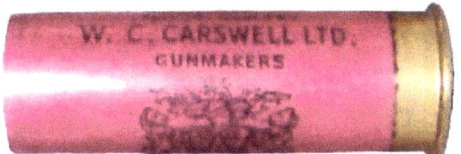 

W. C. CARSWELL LTD. [Gm]. Ad; 4A Chapel St, Liverpool, Lancs.
Kb; The Banshee (shown above), Carswell's Special.

  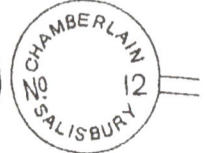

ARTHUR J. CHAMBERLAIN. [Gm, Cl]. Ad; In 1891 and way into the 1930's he was at, 18 Queen St, Salisbury. By 1939 his business had moved to, 21A Milford St, Market Place, Salisbury, Wilts.
Kb; Pinfire, The A.C. County, The A.C. Wiltshire, The Command, Ejector, Pegamoid, The Sarum, Smokeless 410, The Stonehenge, The Wessex, Un.
Rm; At one time he had a premises in Shepton Mallet, Somerset.

 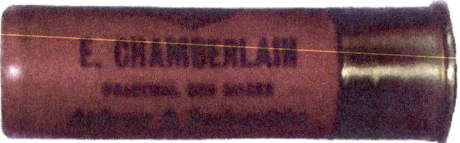 

EDWIN CHAMBERLAIN. [Gm, Cl]. Ad; 1 Bridge St, Andover. Also at, 35 Wote St, Basingstoke, Hants.
Kb; The Smokeless, The Universal, Un.
Rm; Many of his cartridge were not named. His Basingstoke premises were taken Over by Thos Turner & Sons in August 1922. From then on, all business was Conducted from Andover. Any cartridge marked Basingstoke is prior to 1923.

SEPTIMUS CHAMBERS. [Gm]. Ad; 63 Broad St, Bristol, Glos (Avon). Also at, 21 Castle St, Cardiff, Glam. And also at, Shepton Mallet, Som.
Kb; Patent No 15848 (shown above0, Special Smokeless Kynoch Perfectly Gas-tight, Pinfire, Un.

TRADE  MARK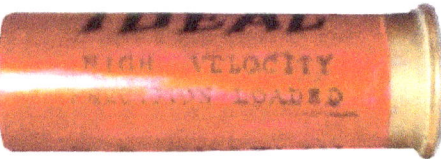

B. E. CHAPLIN. [Gm]. Ad; 6 Southgate St, Winchester, Hants.
Kb; Ideal (shown above), Winton.
Rm; Both Howard A. Davies and Hammond Bros sold a Winton.

R. S. CHITTY.   Ad; 6 Lion St, Chichester, Sussex.
Kb; The Chichester Cross, The Pheasant, The Wonder.
Rm; Cartridges were loaded by Patstone of Southampton.

EDWIN J. CHURCHILL. [Gm,Cl]. Ad; 8 Agar St, The Strand.   Later at, 39-42 Leicester Square, London EC2.
Kb; 8-Points Cartridge, 8-Star, A.G. (accuracy guaranteed), Ejector, ExpressXXV, Churchill's 1935 Cartridge, The Field, The Imperial, Olympic Trapshooting Cartridge, The Pheasant, The Premier, The Prodigy, Special, Special Star, Trapshooting Cartridge, Utility, The Waterproof Metal Lined, Un.

CHARLES CLARKE. [Gs]. Ad; 17 Winchester St, Salisbury, Wilts.
Kb; The Original J.W.G.
Rm; He was known to have had a London premises.

HENRY CLARKE. Later as, H. CLARKE & SONS. [Gm, Cl].
Ad; 38 Gallowtree Gate. Also at, 20 Humberstone Gate, Leicester, Leics.
Kb; The Alma, The Express Cartridge, The Express Special Loading,
The Keeper, The Midland Cartridge, Un.
Rm; The firm was established in 1832.

CLARKE & DYKE. [Gs]. Ad; 17 Winchester St, Salisbury, Wilts. Also at,
Southampton, Hants.
Kb; The J.W.G, The Salisbury.

CLAYTON & SON. [Sports outfitters]. Ad; Huntingdon. Also at, St Neots,
Hunts (Cambs).
Kb; Special British Loaded Cartridge.

 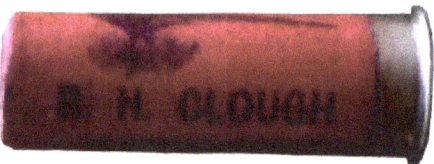 

R. H. CLOUGH.   Ad; 14 Church St, West Hartlepool,
County Durham (Cleveland).
Kb; Un.

THOMAS CLOUGH. Later as, THOS CLOUGH & SON. [Gm].
Ad; 52 High St, King's Lynn, Norfolk.
Kb; The Lynn, The Sandringham, Un.

J.H. COCK & CO. [Gs, Im]. Ad; Market Place, Cirencester, Glos.
Kb; Un.

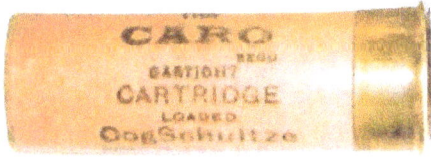

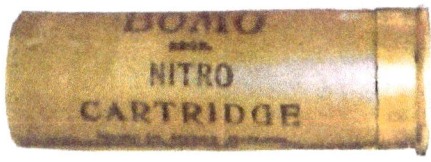 

COGSCHULTZE AMMUNITION & POWDER CO LTD. [Am, Pm].
Ad; The Ammunition Factory, Gillingham St, London SW.
Kb; The Avlo, The Bomo, The Caro, The Farmo, Gastight, The Molto, The Pluvoid, The Ranger, Schultze Smokeless Powder Cartridge, The Torro, The Westro.
Rm; Founded in 1911 using Cogswell & Harrison's cases and Schultze Gunpowder Co's powders. The name Avlo was registered to the firm but may not have been applied to a cartridge. This firm continued into the 1914-18 war.

COGSWELL & HARRISON LTD. [Gm, Cl]. Ad; 141 New Bond St. Also at, 223 The Strand. Later at, 168 Piccadilly, London W1. Was also at, 94 Queen St, Exeter, Devon. Also had a branch in Paris, France.
Kb; The Ardit, The Avant-tout, The Blagdon, The Blagdonette, The Certus, Ejector, The Exceltor, Gastight Cartridge Case, Kynoch's Grouse Ejector, The Huntic, The Kelor, The Konor, The Lined Nitro Cartridge, Markor, The Markoride, The Midget, The New 14¼ Bore (circa 1912), Nitro, Pegamoid, The Smokeless Cartridge, The Stelor, Swiftsure, The Victor, The Victor Universal, The Victoroid, Waterproof Cartridge, Un.
Rm; Founded by Benjamin Cogswell in 1770. Partnered with Edwin Harrison in 1837. In 1932 the firm was liquidated. A new firm emerged in 1933. Their zig-zag markings were registered to them in 1887.

 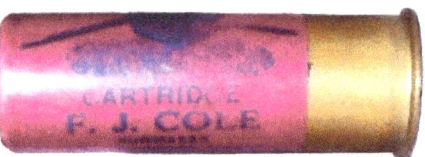 

F. J. COLE LTD. [Gm]. Ad; 171 Cricklade St. Later at, 26 Castle St, Cirencester, Glos.
Kb; The Castle, The Champion, The Crown Favourite, The County Favourite (shown above).
Rm; Circa 1910-14, directories listed him as Cole Fraser Jnr.

FRANK COLE. Later as, COLE & SON. [Gm]. Ad; 14 Market Place. Later at, 33 Market Place, Devizes, Wilts. Also at, 116 Peascod St, Windsor, Berks. Was also at, 21 Pembroke Rd, Portsmouth, Hants. And also at, 89 High St, Cheltenham, Glos.
Kb; The Crown, The Crown Favourite, The Globe, The King Cole, The Royal Cartridge, The Signature.
Rm; Francis John Cole of, 171 Crickdale St, Cirencester was trading at the same Time. Also in 1903 a Mr John Cole was trading from the Market Place in Chippenham, Wilts.

J. COLLIS LTD.   Ad; Strood, Rochester & Gravesend, Kent.
Kb; The All Round, Nullisecundus (also spelt, Nulli Secundus).

 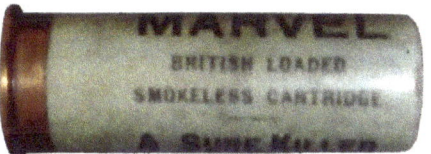 

COLTMAN & CO. [Gm, Cl]. Ad; The Cattle Market. Later at, 49 Station St, Burton-Upon-Trent, Staffs. Also at, Uttoxeter, Staffs, & Ashbourne & Derby, Derbys.
Kb; The Burton, Ejector, The Field, The K.C. (Keepers Cartridge and known as The Staffordshire Knot), The Marvel, Marvel 410, The Partridge, The Rabbit, Pegamoid, The Pheasant. Rm; They loaded, The Governor and The Victor for another firm.

ROY CONWAY.   Ad; Freeman St, Grimsbury, Lincs (Humberside).
Kb; Kynoch's Patent Ejector (14 gauge), Humber Duck & Goose Cartridge.

ARTHUR CONYERS. [Gm, Cl]. Ad; 3 West St, Blandford Forum, Dorset.
Kb; The Dorset County (shown above), Ejector, The Express, The
Express De Luxe, The Marvel 410, Water Resisting Case, Un.
Rm; Arthur was a son of H. Conyers. He started his business in the late
1800's and loaded both pin and centre fire cartridges.

J. E. COOKE.   Ad; Bromyard, Herefs (Hereford & Worcester).
Kb; Un (Cooke's Name on stamping only. Shown above).

J. COOMBES.   Ad; Wheddon Cross, Somerset.
Kb; Champion (shown above), Un.

GEORGE COONEY. [Hardware merchant]. Ad; Cross St-John St Corner, Kells, County Meath, Republic of Ireland.
Kb; Kynoch's Perfectly Gas-tight, Un.
Rm; Business terminated circa 1932-33.

SIDNEY LANCELOT CORDEN. Later as, S. L. CORDEN & SONS. [Im, Cl and Furnishings]. Ad; 37 High St, Warminster, Wilts.
Kb; Quickfire, Special Smokeless, Un.
Rm; Still in business long after the Second World War but no longer loading.

 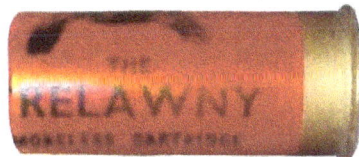 

CORNWALL CARTRIDGE WORKS. [Cl]. Ad; Liskeard, Cornwall.
Kb; The British Challenge, The Cornubia, The Cornwall, The Enterprise, The Tamar, The Trelawney (shown above but cut down to 2 inch).
Rm; Founded by Alfed George Creber of Torcot, Menheniot, Liskeard.

WALTER COTON. [Gs and cartridge expert]. Ad; 153 Foleshill Rd, Coventry, Warwickshire (West Midlands).
Kb; Special Keeper's Cartridge, Un.
Rm; He was blitzed on the raid 14/11/40. He was a crack clay shooter in his time. Many Un yellow tubed with standing cock pheasant were loaded by him.

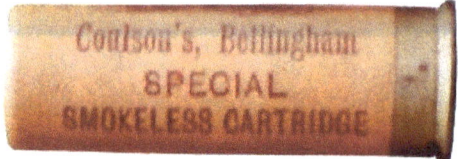 

COULSON.   Ad; Bellingham, Northumberland.
Kb; The Border Cartridge, Special Smokeless.

M. A. COX & SON LTD. [Gm and cutlers]. Ad; 28 High St. Also at, 7 Bernard St, Southampton, Hants.
Kb; J. W. G., The Popular, The Solent, The Southampton Cartridge (shown above), The Star Special Cartridge.
Rm; Established 1830. They were at 7 Bernard St , in 1884.

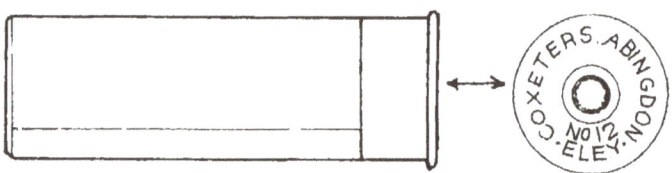

COXETER & SONS. [Im]. Ad; Ock St, Abingdon, Berks (Oxon).
Rm; No known cartridge exists. Provisional drawing made from cartridge remains. They were shown active in a 1887 directory but were not shown in 1895.

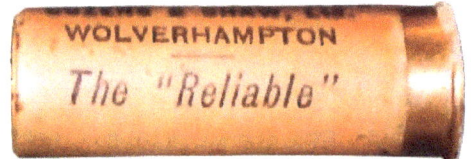 

COZENS & SHAW LTD. [Im]. Ad; 11 Dudley St, Wolverhampton, Staffs (W. Midlands).
Kb; The Reliable.
Rm; Their Ad was taken from a 1896 directory.

D. CROCKART & SONS. Later as, D. CROCKART & CO. [Gm rifle and fishing tackle]. Ad; 35 King St, Stirling, Stirlingshire (Central).
Kb; The Crockart, Ejector, The Grampion, The Stirling, Un (shown Above).

 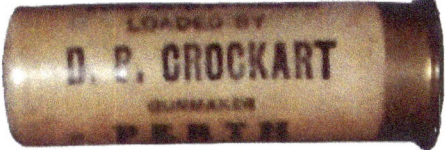 

D. B. CROCKART. [Gm and fishing tackle]. Ad; 33-35 County Place, Perth, Perthshire (Tayside).
Kb; The Perth Cartridge, The Spotfinder, The True Line.

JAS CROCKART & SON. [Gm rifle and fishing tackle]. Ad; 26 Allen St, Blairgowrie, Perthshire (Tayside).
Kb; The J. C. & S. (shown above).
Rm; Established in 1852.

S. B. CROSS. [Explosives dealers]. Ad; 183 Price St. Also at, Chester St, Birkenhead, Ches (Merseyside).
Kb; Un.

CURTIS'S & HARVEY LTD. [Pm, Am]. Ad; 3 Gracechurch St. Also at, Cannon Street House, London EC.
Kb; Amberite, Ejector, Feather Weight, Gastight, Lined Nitro, The Marvel, Ruby, Smokeless Diamond, Unlined Nitro.
Rm; C & H eventually amalgamated with John Hall & Son.

DANIEL & MORRIS. [Agricultural Im]. Ad; St Clears, Carm (Dyfed).
Kb; The Victor (shown above, pictures a running rabbit).

WALTER DARLOW. Later as, W. DARLOW & CO. [Gm, Im]. Ad; 27 Midland Rd, Bedford, Beds. Later at, Orford Hill, Norwich, Norfolk.
Kb; 20 Gauge, The Big Bag, The Castle, The Lightning (shown above), The Orford, The Special, Special Gastight, Special Red Gastight.
Rm; Listed in a 1894 directory as both Gm and Im.

DATE BROTHERS. [Sports depot]. Ad; Frome, Somerset.
Kb; The County Cartridge for Fur and Feather.

 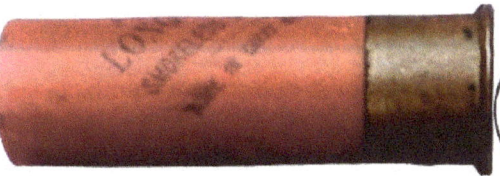 

JAMES A. DAVIDSON. [Cl, wine and spirit merchant].
Ad; Wells-next-the-Sea, Norfolk.
Kb; Joyce's Long Brass Smokeless (Davidson on top card only), The New Era.

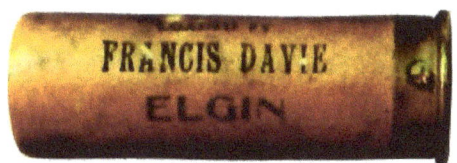 

FRANCIS DAVIE. [Gm]. Ad; 153 High St, Elgin, Moray (Grampian).
Kb; The Moray Cartridge, Un.

HOWARD A. DAVIES. [Gm]. Ad; 6 Southgate St, Winchester, Hants.
Kb; The Flight, The Winton.
Rm; This business got taken over by, B. E. Chaplin. The Winton being a shortened name for Winchester.

 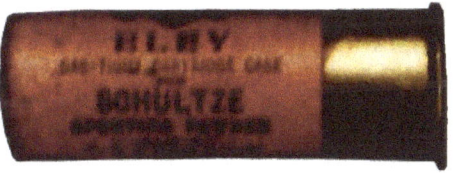 

F. DAWSON.   Ad; Altringham, Ches (Great Manchester).
Kb; Eley's Gas-tight Cartridge Case for Schultze Sporting Powder (Dawson's name on the top card only), Kleenkiller.

JOHN T. DICKINS. [Im]. Ad; 69 Bridge St, Northampton, Northants.
Kb; Kynoch 5/8" Brass (name on over shot card), Nobel Gas-tight Cartridge Case (name on over shot card).

JOHN DICKSON & SON LTD. [Gm]. Ad; 20 Royal Exchange. Also at, 21 Frederick St, Edinburgh, Midlothian. Was also in Glasgow and Kelso-on-Tweed, Roxburgh.
Kb; The Capital, Ejector, Dickson's Favourite, The Jubilee, Dickson's Pegamoid, The Special Blue Shell, Rabbit Cartridge, Pinfire, Un.

R. DOTT THOMSON. [Im and cycle agent]. Ad; 1-2 Cross, Cupar, Fife.
Kb; Special Smokeless Cartridge.

JAMES D. DOUGALL & SONS. [Gm and rifle]. Ad; 52 Argyle Arcade St. Also at, 88 and 177 Trongate. Also at, 23 and 39 Gordon St. Also at, 3 West Nile St. Also at, 18A-18B Renfield St. Also at, 4 Bothwell St. And Also at, 10 Waterloo St, Glasgow, Lanarks (Strathclyde).
Kb; Ejector, Pegamoid Special Loading, Un. Rm, Were also in London.

 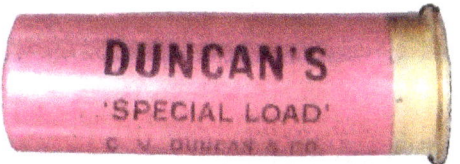 

STANLEY DUNCAN & SONS. Later as, C. V. DUNCAN & CO. [Gm].
Ad; 62 Anlaby Rd, Hull, Yorks (Humberside).
Kb; Duncan's Special Load (shown above), The Duncan Special.
Rm; This firm later became, Duncan (Gunmakers) Ltd, at 8 Paragon Square, in Hull.

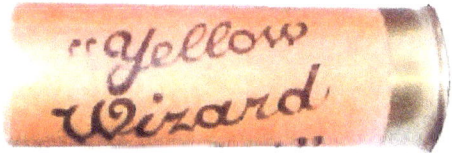 

FRANK DYKE & CO LTD. [Cl, Wm]. Ad; 10 Union St, London SE. Also at, 6-7 St George's Avenue, London EC. And also at, 1-7 Ernest Avenue, West Norwood, London SE.
Kb; Frank Dyke's Supreme, Rabbit Cartridge, Shamrock, Shamrock 410, Special, Special Gastight, Yellow Wizard, Yellow Wizard Rustless, Un.
Rm; Loaded for other firms country wide. Used German made cases and components. Not all of their brands carried their own name.

 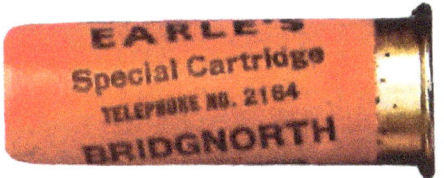 

G. A. EARLE. [Im]. Ad; Bridgnorth, Shropshire.
Kb; Earle's Special Cartridge (shown above).

REYNOLDS RICHARD EARLE. [Im.].
Ad; High Street, Hungerford, Berks.
Cr; 1877-1887. Nt; No street number known.
Remains found by metal detecting.

Nt; Findings had 8 mm brass head.
There is no known cartridge.

EAST ESSEX FARMERS LTD. [Id]. Ad; Maldon & Southend, Essex.
Kb; 3.E.S. (shown above).

THE E. C. POWDER CO LTD. [Cl, Pm]. Ad; 20 Bucklersbury.
Also at, 40 New Broad St, London EC.
Kb; E.C., E. C. Pegamoid, Eley's Ejector.
Rm; The company got confused with other powder manufactures and so they
Arrived at using the letters E.C.

F. R. EDGAR.   Longtown, Cumberland (Cumbria).
Kb; Un.

EDNIE & KININMONTH. [Im and seed merchants]. Ad; Forfar, Angus (Tayside).
Kb;Un.

AUBREY EDWARDS & CO LTD.　　　　Ad; 32 Oxford St, Swansea, Glam.
Kb; The Eclipse, The Gower.

EDWARDS LTD. [Gs, Cl]. Ad; Newport , Monmouthshire (Gwent).
Kb; The Champion, The Newport.

  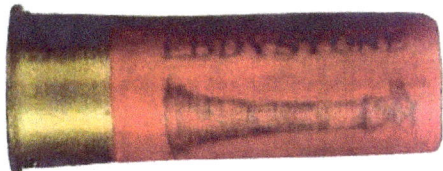

C. G. EDWARDS & SON. [Gm or Gs]. Ad; 2 George St. Also at, Frankfort Lane, Plymouth, Devon.
Kb; The Eddystone, The Smeaton.

ELEY BROTHERS, LTD. [Am, Wm]: Ad; 254 Gray's Inn Road, London WC4. Works at; Angel Road, Edmonton, London N18. [Am, Wm].
Kb Muzzle Loading Patent Wire; The Green (green), The Royal (red). Kb Muzzle Loading no wire; The Universal (yellow).
Kb Pinfire; (blue), Brown Quality (brown), Green Extra Quality (green), Red Quality (red).
Kb Central Fire Early Brands; Ejector (extended brass), The E.B. Nitro Case, Improved Gas'tight (Also known as The E.B.L.), Pegamoid (used special Pegamoid waterproof paper), Solid drawn Brass, Thin Brass, Kb For Individual Powders; Hall's Smokeless Cannonite (red), Amberite (grey), Cooppal Smokeless Game(red), Cooppal No 2 (maroon), 'E.C' (red), Shot Gun Rifleite (red), Sporting Ballistite (cream-yellow), 'S.S' Smokeless (grey).
This firm also advertised Short Smokeless. Kb; Lancaster's Pygmies (red), The Midget, The Parvo, Tom Thumb, Un.
Kb Later Brands; The 3/8" Shell Gastight, Achilles, Acme, Aquoid, Beacon, Black Twenty (20 Gg), Comet, Coralite Smokeless (Australian market), Damp Proof (two piece half rolled brass), 'D.S', The E.B.L, E.B. Nitro Case, Ecar, Ejector, Eleite, Eley Smokeless, Eloid, Erin-Go-Bragh, Express, Fourlong (410), Fourten (410), Gastight, Gastight Deep Shell Unlined, Grand Prix, Improved Gastight, Juno, Lab Case (Proofhouse only), Lightmode, Lined Nitro Ball, Nitro Case, Mars, Neptune, Pardo Smokeless, Pegamoid, Pigeon Cartridge, Pluto, Quail (sold in Australia), Rocket, The S.A, Thor, Titan, Universal, The V.C, Vulcan, Zenith, Un..
Rm; This firm was known active in 1828. It printed JOB lot cartridges and Sold very many brands and empty case for small firms. It also had overseas Addresses and traded worldwide. In 1918 it merged into the new large firm of Explosive Trades Ltd (E.T.L.). They also made the small and large gauges and also for punt guns.

EDWARDS & MELUISH.
Ad; Harborne, Birmingham, Warw (West Midlands).
Kb; The Edmel Smokeless (shown above).

ELDERKIN & SON. [Gs]. Ad; Spalding, Lincs.
Kb; The Premier (shown above).

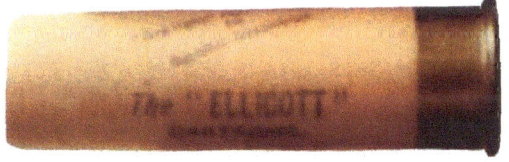 

ELLICOTT.   Ad; Cardiff, South Glamorgan.
Kb; The Ellicott Cartridge (Gastight Cartridge Case for Schultze Gunpowder), Cone Based Case (patent No 14814).

H. C. ELLIOTT. [Gm]. Ad; Lowfield St, Dartford, Kent.
Kb; The Smasher.

ELTON STORES LTD. [Ds]. Ad; 140 Coniscliffe Rd, Darlington, County Durham.
Kb; Competition (shown above), Pest Control, Standard, Trapshooting.
Rm; Cartridges were closed by rolled turn-over and six fold crimp.

ELVEDEN ESTATE. [Es]. Ad; Elveden Hall, Near Thetford, Suffolk.
Kb; Elveden Estate (shown above).

ENGLAND & SONS. Ad; Parliament St, Harrogate, Yorks. [Im].
Kb; Un.

 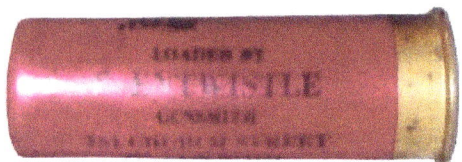 

S. ENTWHISTLE. [Gs]. Ad; 151 Church St, Blackpool, Lancs.
Kb; The Blackpool Special, Un.

WILLIAM EVANS. [Gm]. Ad; 63 Pall Mall, London EC.
Kb; 20 Bore, 16 Bore, Ejector, Gastight, High Velocity, Mark Over, Marlboro, Pall Mall, Pegamoid, Sky High.
Rm; This firm was known to have been active from the above address as early as 1908.

Many of the merged firms brand names were kept. Note the initials ETL on the Bonax and the Primax.

EXPLOSIVES TRADES LTD. [Am, Pm, Cl]. Ad; Witton, Birmingham, Warw (W. Midlands). Rm; Formed in the November 1918 with the merger of many firms. It continued for two years as E.T.L. and then changed its name to NOBEL INDUSTRIES LTD. For information on their cartridges, see this name in this book.

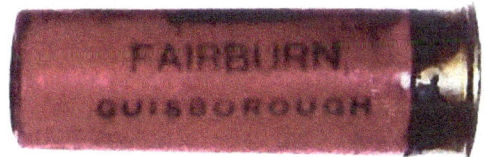

FAIRBURN. Ad; Guisborough, Yorks (Cleveland).
Kb; Un.

BRYAN FARRELLY & SON.   Ad; Castle St, Kells, County Antrim, Northern Ireland.
Kb; Kenlis (shown above).

FREDERICK S. FLETCHER. Also was, MRS E. FLETCHER. Later as, E. FLETCHER & SONS. [Gm]. Ad; I have several but do not know their order In time. 158 Westgate St; 18 Westgate St; 20-24 King's Square, Gloucester. Also at, 92 Winchcombe St, Cheltenham, Glos.
Kb; The Gloucester, The Pheasant, Un.

 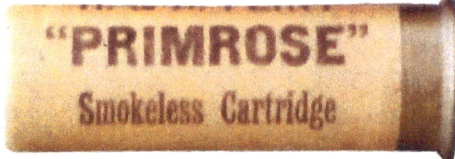 

H & A. FLINT.　　　　Ad; Hemel Hempstead, Herts.
Kb; Primrose Smokeless Cartridge.

G. FODEN.　　Ad; Openshaw, Manchester, Lancs (Gt Manchester).
Kb; Eley's Gastight Case for Curtis''s & Harvey's Smokeless Diamond (Foden's name on top card. Shown above).

FOLLETT.　　　Ad; Colyton & Seaton, Devon.
Kb; Un (Follett name on the stamping or over shot card).

WILLIAM FORD. [Gm]. Ad; Eclipse Works, 15 St Mary's Row. Also at, 4 Price St. And also at, 96 Potters Hill, Aston, Birmingham, Warw (W. Midlands).
Kb; The Eclipse, The Fleet, Patent Ignition Tube (shown above)., Special British.

 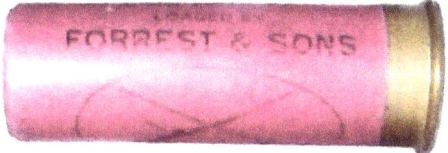 

FORREST & SONS. [Gm and dealers]. Ad; 35 The Square, Kelso-on-Tweed, Roxburghs (Borders).
Kb; The Border Smokeless, The County, The Tweed.

A.J.FOSTER. {Gs}. Ad; Sheffield House, 16 The Bull Ring, Kidderminster, Worcs (H & W).
Kb; Empire Cartridge, Field Cartridge, The Quick Hit, Un.

ISAAC FOX. Later as, CECIL FOX. [Gm]. Ad; 4 Upper Bridge St, Canterbury, Kent.
Kb; The County Cartridge (shown above), Kynoch Gastight, Un.
Rm; Both Isaac and Cecil sold the County. Later this business was run by H. S. Greenfield & Son who continued to market The County Cartridge.

 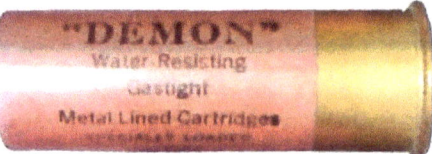 

CHARLES FRANCIS. Later as, C. FRANCIS & SONS. Later still as, C. FRANCIS & SON. [Gm]. Ad; Long Causeway, Peterborough, Northants (Cambs). Kb; The Demon (shown above), The Reliable, The Reliance, Schultze.

FRANCIS & DEAN. [Gs]. Ad; 8 St Mary's Hill, Stamford, Lincs. Kb; Hy-Bird (shown above).

J. W. FRANK. Ad; Guisborough, Yorks (Cleveland). Kb; Un.

DANIEL FRASER & CO. [Gm]. Ad; 4 Leith St Terrace, Edinburgh, Midlothian. Kb; Pegamoid, Un.

EDWARD FROST. Ad; Bridlington, Yorks (Humberside).
Kb; Un.

JONN FRY. [Gm]. Ad; 17 Sadlergate, Derby, Derbys.
Kb; The Derby Cartridge (shown above).

FUSSELL'S LTD. [Gm]. Ad; 118-119 Cheap Side, London EC2. Also at, 53 Cross St, Abergavenny, Mont (Gwent). Also at, 81 Station Rd, Port Talbot, West Glamorgan. And also at, 2 Dock St & Market Buildings, Newport, Mon (Gwent).
Kb; The Club (shown above).

EDWARD GALE. Later as, E. GALE & SONS LTD. [Gm]. Ad; 20 Joy St, Barnstaple. Also at, 2-3 Mill St, Bideford, Devon.
Kb; Castle, County, Farm Cartridge, The Field, The Flag, The Hawk (410), Pegamoid, Unlined Nitro, The X.L. (shown above).

GALLYON & SONS LTD. [Gm]. Ad; 66 Bridge St, Cambridge, Cambs. Also at, 52 High St, King's Lynn, Norfolk. Later at, 5 Cowgate, Peterborough, Northants (Cambs). And also at, 9-11 Bedford St, Norwich, Norfolk.
Kb; The A.C.M, The Camroid, The Camrose, The Club Cartridge, The Cooppal Express, Granton, Kilham, Lynton, Newgun, Sandringham, Super Vanguard, The Vanguard, Un.

 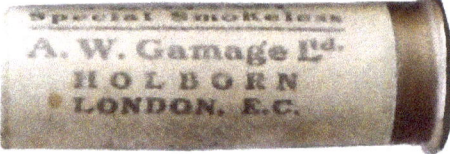 

A. W. GAMAGE LTD. [Ds, Gs]. Ad; Holborn, London EC1.
Kb; The A.W.G., The Corona, The Holborn, The Referee, Special Smokeless.

JOHN G. GAMBLE. [Am]. Ad; Magherafelt, Londonderry, Northern Ireland.
Kb; Swift (drawing shown above).

GAMEBORE CARTRIDGE CO LTD. [Cartridge makers].
Ad; Great Union Street, Hull, Yorks (Humberside).
Kb; Black Powder.
Rm; A very modern firm when compared with the majority in this book. The decision to show this was as it was closed by a card with a paper tube.

 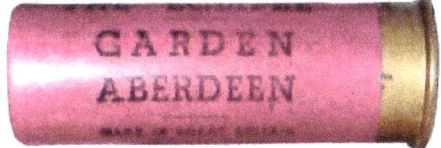 

WILLIAM GARDEN. [Gm]. Ad; 122 Union St, Aberdeen, Aberdeens (Grampian).
Kb; The Eclipse (shown above), Gastight, The Granite City, Special Brown.

T. M. GARDINER LTD. [Ammunition Dealer]. Ad; Hoddeson, Herts.
Kb; Un.

FRANK GARRETT. [Gm or Gs, Cl]. Ad; Bath St, Birmingham. Also at, Ilmington, Nr Stratford-upon-Avon, Warw. Later at, Evesham, Worcs (H & W).
Kb; Blue Flash Pigeon Cartridge, Crimson Flash, The D.B.H. (Deadly but humane), Flash Junior (410), Golden Flash, Tempest.

E. GIBBS & SON. Ad; Reepham, Norfolk. [Im].
Kb; The Reepham Cartridge.

GEORGE GIBBS LTD. [Gm or Gs]. Ad; 37 Baldwin St. Also at, 39 Corn St.
Also at, St John's Bridge, Bristol, Glos (Avon). And also, 35 Saville Row, London W1.
Kb; The Bristol, The County, The Covert, The Crown, The Farm Cartridge,
The Field, The Gibbs, The Intermediate, Kynoch 5/8" Brass, Un.

GIFFORD.   Ad; Wincanton, Somerset.
Kb; Not known.
Rm; The above provisional drawing has been made from
metal detected remains.

JOHN H. GILL.   Ad; Danby, Yorks.
Kb; The Tyke (on a Mullerite).

J. GILMAN & SONS LTD.   Ad; The Corner, Stratford St & Corporation St, Birmingham, Warw (W. Midlands).
Kb; Un (registered No, 28596).

J. GLIDDON & SONS. [Hardware, agricultural].
Ad; Willington & Minehead, Som.
Kb; The Exmoor Cartridge
Rm; Gliddon took over the business of William Tarr & Sons in 1913. Tarr had also marketed an Exmoor Cartridge.

W. GODFREY & SONS.   Ad; Yeovil, Som.
Kb; Special Smokeless.

 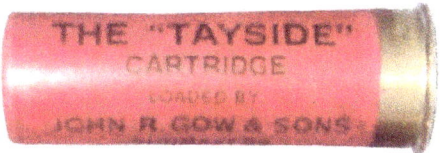 

JOHN R. GOW & SONS. [Gm]. Ad; 12 Union St, Dundee, Angus (Tayside).
Kb; The Tayside, Un.

GEORGE P. GRAHAM. [Gm]. Ad; Station St, Cockermouth, Cumberland (Cumbria).
Kb; The Cumberland (shown above), The Skiddaw.

JOHN GRAHAM & CO LTD. [Gm]. Ad; 27 Union St, Inverness, Inverness-shire (Highland).
Kb; Bon-ton, Eley Ejector, The Highland, Pegamoid, The Primo, Special.

GRANT & LANG. (STEPHEN GRANT & JOSEPH LANG LTD). [Gm].
Ad; 7 & 8 Bury St, St James, London SW1.
Kb; The Briton, The Curzon, The Grantbury, The Instanter, Pegamoid, Rocketer, The Velogrant.   Rm; Founded in 1925. They incorporated Charles Lancaster and Watson Bros. Active unti 1960. Joined with Henry Atkin.

D. GRAY & CO. [Gm]. Ad; 30 Union St. Later at, 14 Union St, Inverness, Inverness-shire (Highland).
Kb; Autokill (shown above), Bas Cinteach, Gastight, The Mors, Pegamoid, Waterproof.

REGINALD GRAY. [Sports dealer]. Ad; Doncaster, Yorks. Kb; The Don.

EDWISON C. GREEN. Later as, EDWINSON GREEN & SONS. [Gm]. Ad; 4 Northgate St, Gloucester. Also at, 87 High St, Cheltenham, Glos. Kb; The Cotswold, Fur & Feather, Maxim, S.P. (Special Smokeless), The Velox Cartridge.

WILLIAM WELLINGTON GREENER. Became, W.W. GREENER LTD. [Gm and Rifle maker]. Ad; St Mary's Square, Birmingham, Warw (W. Midlands). Also at, 68 Haymarket, London SW. Also at, Trinity House Lane, Hull, Yorks (Humberside). Kb; Dead Shot, Ejector, Greener's Dwarf, Gamekeeper, Police Gun E-K, Punt Gun, Sporting Life, Un. Rm; The firm was active between 1860-1966. Also overseas.

 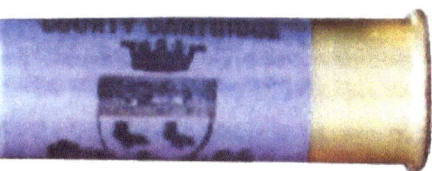 

H. S. GREENFIELD & SON. {Gm and rifle]. Ad; 4 Upper Bridge St. Later at, 5 Dover St, Canterbury, Kent.
Kb; The County Cartridge.
Rm; Greenfield took over 4 Upper Bridge St, from Gm, Cecil Fox.

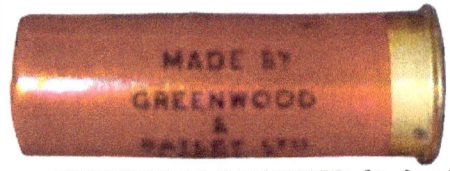  

GREENWOOD & BATLEY LTD. [Am]. Ad; The Albion Works, Leeds.
Also at, Farnham, Yorks.
Kb; A.E.C. Grey Squirrel, A.E.C. Pest Control, The Greenwood, The Skyrack, Standard Load, Trapshooting Cartridge, Trapshooting Load.
Rm; Only made in 12 gauge with crimson or orange paper tubes.

 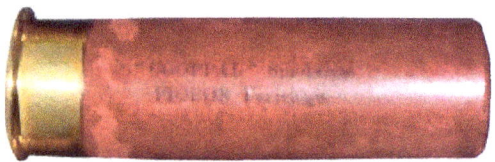

GRENFELL & ACCLES. [Cartridge case manufacturers, Cl].
Ad; Perry Bar, Birmingham, Warw (West Midlands).
Kb; Cooppal Smokeless Pigeon Cartridge (shown above), Un.
Rm; This firm was dissolved in 1896.

FRANK HALL. [Gs]. Ad; 9 Beetwell St, Chesterfield, Derbys.
Kb; Hallrite Special (shown above).
Rm; All of these that I have seen had poor tube printings.

HUGH HALL. [Gm and stores]. Ad; Wetherby, Yorks.
Kb; The Farmer's Stores, Un.
Rm; Hugh sold Kynoch & Co brands, circa 1908-9.

 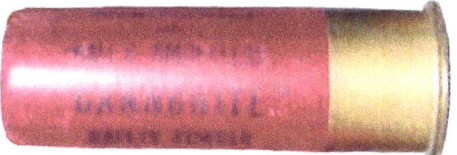 

JOHN HALL & SON. [Pm]. Ad; 79 Cannon St, London EC4.
Kb; Hall's Cannonite, Hall's Field B, Southern Cross.
Rm; Cartridges took their names from the firms powders.

B. HALLIDAY & CO LTD. [Gm]. Ad; 60 Queen Victoria St. Later at, 63 Cannon St, London EC4.
Kb; The City, The Express, High Velocity, Pheasant, Stopem.
Rm; This firm started trading in London in 1922.

HAM & HUDDY. [Jewlers and game dealers]. Ad; 19 Fore St, Liskeard, Cornwall.
Kb; Un (shown above, their name was on the over shot card).
Rm; Their name has also been seen on stampings on cartridge remains.

HAMMOND BROS. [Gm]. Ad; 40 Jewry St, Winchester, Hants.
Kb; Ejector, Reliance, Trusty Servant, Winton (shown above), Yellow Seal Mullerite.
Rm; The firm moved to 48 Bridge St, Andover, Hants, in the mid1960's.

W. T. HANCOCK. [Gm]. Ad; 308 High Holborn, London WC1.
Kb; Kynoch's Perfectly Gas-tight (shown above).

J. HARDING.   Ad; Benfleet, Thames Estuary, Essex.
Kb; Eley Bros Blue Quality (Harding's name on over shot card only. Shown above).

HARDY BROS LTD. [Gm]. Ad; London and North British Works, Alnwick, Nthmb. Also at, 69 George St, Edinburgh. Also at, 117 West George St, Glasgow. Also at, 12 Moult St, Manchester. And also at, 61 Pall Mall, London SW.   Kb; Hardy's Hotspur, Hardy's Northern, Hardy's Northern High Velocity, Hardy's Reliance.

JOHN CHARLES HARDY. [Gm or Gs]. Ad; West End, Holbeach, R.S.O., Lincs.
Kb; The Holbeach Long Range Cartridge.

JOSEPH HARKOM & SON. Later as, J. HARKOM & SONS LTD. [Gm].
Ad; 50 George St, Edinburgh, Midlothian.
Kb; Ejector (shown above).

GEORGE & A. HARRIS. [Im]. Ad; Market Place, Uttoxeter, Staffs.
Kb; Yew-Tox, Un.

HARRODS LTD. [Ds]. Ad; Brompton Rd,
Knightsbridge, London SW1.
Kb; The Beaufort, The British Pioneer, Hurlingham,
The Kill-Sure, The Pioneer.

FREDERICK W. HART. [Gm]. Ad; 39 Queen St. Also at King St,
Scarborough, Yorks.
Kb; The Crackshot, The Eclipse, The Express (shown above),
The Marvel 410, The Rocket.

A. B. HARVEY.   Ad; 1-2 The Strand, Falmouth, Cornwall.
Kb; The Strand (shown above), Un.

COLIN H. HAYGARTH. [Cl, Gt]. Ad; The Cottage Gunshop, Dunnet, Caithness.
Kb; The Economax.
Rm; Colin and his son went on to load other brands but with crimped closure.

HAYMAN.   Ad; Dorchester. Also at Weymouth, Dorset.
Kb; Nk.
Rm; Research has not traced this firm or its type of business.. The above provisional drawings are from metal detected remains.

WILLIAM HAYNES. [Im]. Ad; 19 Duke St. Also at, High Bridge Wharf, King's Rd, Reading, Berks.
Kb; Nk.
Rm; The above provisional drawing has been made from metal Detected cartridge remains.

HAYWARD & SONS. [Im]. Ad; 125-126 High St, Tewkesbury, Glos. Also at, New St, Upton-on-Severn, Worcs (Hereford & Worcester).
Kb; Un.
Rm; Directories show them as active in Tewkesbury circa 1910-1919 and active in Upton circa 1921.

MRS SARAH HAZEL. [Im]. Ad; 15 High West St. Also, Trinity St. Also, Prince's St. And also at, Great Western Rd, Dorchester, Dorset.
Kb; Nk.   Rm; The above provisional drawing has been made from cartridge remains. Hazel was known to have been active between 1880 and 1895. A 1907 directory gave Im Walley & Windows at 15 High West St.

WALTER ERNEST HEAL. Later as, W. E. HEAL LTD. [Im].
Bampton St, Tiverton, Devon.
Kb; The Special Rabbit Cartridge, The Supa Tivvy, The Tivvy, Tivvy Super.

HELLIS-ROSSON LTD. [Gm, Cl]. Ad; 7 Bedford St, Norwich, Norfolk.
Kb; Economist, Kuvert.
Rm; Most of their brands were crimp closed.

CHARLES HELLIS. Later as, CHARLES HELLIS & SONS LTD. [Cl].
Ad; 119 Edgware Rd. Later at, 121-3 Edgware Rd, Hyde Park West, London W2.
Kb; 12 X 2", 12 X 2" Deep Shell, Aladix, Aldix Ventura, The Championship, Damp Proof, The Economist, Economy, The Edgware, The Falcon, The G.A. (Guaranteed Accuracy), Gas-tight, The Kestrel, Kynoch Grouse Ejector, The Merlin, Pegamoid, The Service, The Standard, The Woodcock, Un.
Rm; Established 1884. This firm loaded for many firms and private people which included royalty. Aldix and Astral may have been names for other firms. On their over-shot cards they used the wordings, Guaranteed Accuracy. Were known to have loaded in gauges 12, 16 and 20. Not all of their brands carried the brand name. They finally closed their doors in 1956 and merged with Rosson's of Norwich and then became Hellis-Rosson Ltd.

J. HELSON. Ad; 84 Fore St, Exeter, Devon.
Kb; The Demon (shown above), The Invincible, Victor.

WALTER HEMING. [Im]. Ad; High St, Wickham. Also at, Fareham, Hants.
Kb; The Meon Valley Special Smokeless (Shown above).

HENRITE EXPLOSIVES. [Cl, Pm]. Ad; Office at, 97 Wilton Rd, London SW. Factory and powder mills at, Dartford, Kent.
Kb; Ejector, The Henrite (shown above), Pigeon Cartridge.
Rm; The name Henrite was registered in 1889 to Luck's Explosives Ltd. This firm was active at least until 1907. Cartridges were sold in both 12 and 16 gauge.

ALEXANDER HENRY. Later as, ALEXANDER HENRY & CO. [Gm]. Ad; 18 Frederick St. Also at, 12 Andrew St, Edinburgh, Midlothian. Was also at, 23 Pall Mall, London SW1.
Kb; Un (shown above).
Rm; Was active between 1902-1939. Merged with Alex Martin Ltd.

THOMAS HEPPLESTONE. [Gm]. Ad; 25 Shudehill, Manchester, Lancs (Great Manchester).
Kb; Kynoch Grouse Ejector, Un (shown above).

 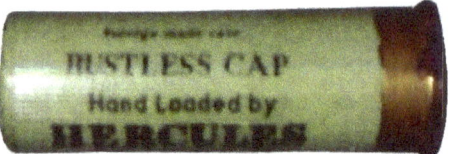 

HERCULES ARMS CO LTD. [Gun and cartridge dealers]. Ad; 8 St Martin's St, Leicester Square, London WC2.
Kb; The Farm Cartridge, The Hercules, Waterproof.
Rm; This firm shared premises with E. J. Churchill. It was a corner building of the joining of two streets and having two Ad.

W. HERRING.   Ad; Street, Somerset.
Kb; Special Smokeless.

 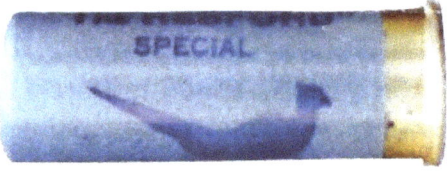 

CHARLES M. HESFORD & CO LTD. [Impliment dealers].
Ad; Ormskirk, Lancs.
Kb; The Hesford Special.

GEORGE G. HIGHAM. [Gm, Fishing tackle maker, Cycle agent and sports].
Ad; 3 Bailey St, Oswestry. Also at, 20 Berriew St, Welshpool, Mont.
Kb; The Eclipse, Eley Ejector, Hios, Pegamoid, Velox.
Rm; Established 1825 long before shotgun cartridges.

W. R. HINDE.   Ad; Whitehaven, Cumberland (Cumbria).
Kb; Special Smokeless Cartridge.

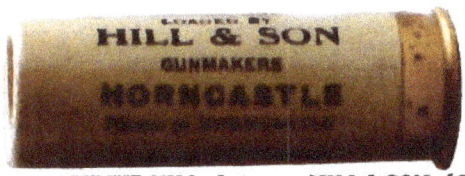  

ARTHUR HILL. Later as, HILL & SON. [Gm]. Ad; 9 Market Place,
Horncastle, Lincs.
Kb; The Champion, The County Cartridge, The Ideal, The Reliable.
Rm; Arthur took over from the Gm, Geoffrey H.Wilson at the above Ad
in 1902. Wilson had also sold a Champion cartridge.

 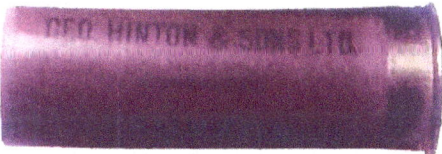 

GEORGE HINTON & SONS LTD. [Gm]. Ad; 5 Fore St, Taunton, Somerset.
Kb; Hinton's Eclipse Gamekeepers, Special I.X.L., The Standard, The
Taunton, Un.
Rm; Established 1815. The Standard dates from 1918. The business changed
Hands in 1947.

HARRY HIGGINS.   Ad; 46-48 Theme St, Tenbury Wells,
Worcestershire (Hereford & Worcester).
Kb; The Dead Shot, Harry Higgins Special (shown above).

RUSSELL HILLSDON. [Gun and field sports]. Ad; Chichester, Horsham & Worthing, Sussex. Also in Birmingham, Warw (W. Midlands) & Farnham, Surrey.
Kb; The Combat, The Goodwood, The Revenge, The Sussex Champion, The Sussex Express, Un.
Rm; Their Farnham shop opened in 1921.

H. M. GOVERNMENT OF GREAT BRITAIN. [Armed services and civil Departments]. Ad; The Houses of Parliament, Westminster SW1.
Kb; A.E.C. Pest Control, A.E.C. Rook Cartridge, Agricultural Departments Reserve, Eley Rocket Cartridge, Eley Trapshooting Cartridge, Forestry Commision Pest Control, L.G., S.G., W.A.E.C. Grey Squirrel, Un, etc.
Rm; Due to World War Two, our government ordered many shotgun types of cartridges.. These were used for training gunnery, engine starting, signal flares and for cutting balloon cables. Other departments ordered cartridges for general pest controlling such as squirrels and rabbits etc.

JOHN HOBSON. [Gm]. Ad; 63 Regent St, Leamington Spa, Warw.
Kb; The Challenge (shown above), The Dead Shot, Hobson's Choice, Hobson's Full Stop, Kynoch Grouse Ejector.

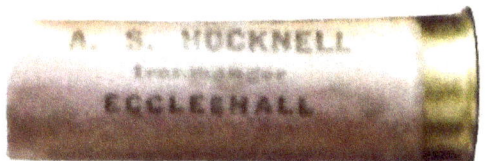 

A.S. HOCKNELL. [Im]. Ad; Eccleshall, Staffs.
Kb; Un.

HENRY HODGSON. [Gm]. Ad; 4 The Traverse, Bury St Edmunds.
Also at, 6 Northgate St, Ipswich, Suffolk.
Kb; The County De-Luxe, The Eclipse, The Express, The Klean Kill Gastight, The Orwell, Pegamoid, The Perfect, The Special, The Suffolk, Waterproof Cartridge.

WILLIAM HODGSON. [Gm]. Ad; 8 Middle St, Ripon, Yorks.
Kb; Eley Blue Quality Case, The Rapido, Special Smokeless, Un (shown above).
Rm; R. C. Hodgson and William Hodgson were both based in Ripon and both of them sold Rapido cartridges.

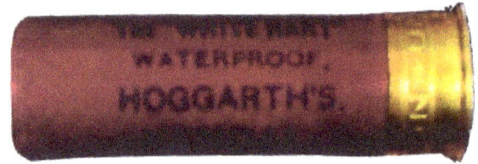 

HOGGARTH.   Ad; Kendal, Westmorland (Cumbria).
Kb; The White Hart.

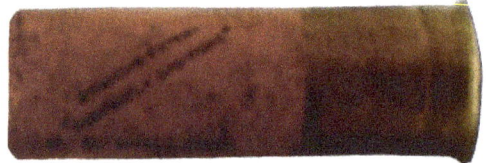 

CHARLES R. HOLLAND. [Gm]. Ad; 43 Dollar St, Cirencester, Glos.
Kb; The Nonsuch Smokeless Cartridge (Kynock Perfectly Gas-tight)
Rm; In 1870 David Holland occupied the above Ad. Charles was known
Active circa 1885-1889 at No 43 and perhaps for much longer.

HOLLAND & HOLLAND LTD. [Gm and rifle]. Ad; 98 New Bond St, London W1.
Kb; The Badminton, The Badminton High Velocity Large Cap, The Centenary
Cartridge, The Dominion, Ejector, High Velocity, Nitro Ball, Nitro Paradox,
Pegamoid, Recoilite, Rewa (4 gauge), The Royal, The Twelve-Two, Two Gauge,
Un.   Rm; The Royal had an inner metal liner with a crimped closure.

HOLTOM'S.   Ad; 243 London Rd (South), Lowestoft, Suffolk.
Kb; Un.

THEODORE J. HOOKE. Later as, T. J. HOOKE & SONS. [Gm].
A d; 38-39 The Pavement, Coppergate, York, Yorks.
Kb; Ebor Cartridge 410 (shown above), Eclipse Cartridge, The Gimcrack,
Hooke's Imperial. Rm; Two other York Ad's for this firm were, 28-30 Coppergate
And 20 Clarance St. J. A. Hooke was the Gm at the above Ad in 1904.

WILLIAM M. HOOTON. [Gm]. Ad, 15 South Gate, Sleaford, Lincs.
Kb; Eley E.B. Nitro Case (Hooton's name on the over shot card only,
Special Smokeless Cartridge (shown above).

HOOTON & JONES. [Gm]. Ad; 60 Dale St, Liverpool, Lancs (Merseyside).
Kb; Hooton & Jones's Special, The Smokeless Cartridge.

J. J. HOPKINS LTD. [Im]. Ad; 2-4 Lake St, Leighton Buzzard, Beds.
Kb; The Golden Pheasant Special Smokeless (shown above).

 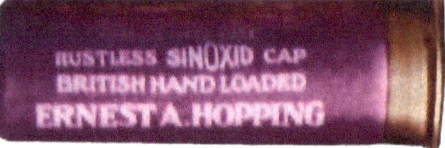 

ERNEST ALFRED HOPPING. [Im]. Ad; 5 Monmouth St, Lostwithiel, Cornwall.
Kb; The Rabbit Cartridge.

THOMAS HORSLEY. Later as, T. HORSLEY & SONS LTD. [Gm]. Ad; 10 Coney St. Later at, Micklegate, York, Yorks.
Kb; Smokeless Rabbit Cartridge, Un.

WILLIAM HORTON. [Gm, rifle and fishing tackle]. Ad; 29 Union St. Later at, 11 Royal Exchange Square. Later still at, 98 Buchanan St. Also at 119 Buchanan St, Glasgow, Lanark (Strathclyde). Rm; Established in 1855.
Kb; Eley's Ejector, Eley Patent Gas-tight (Horton's name on wad and stamping, shown above), The Extra, The Horton Cartridge, Waterproof.

HOWES & SON. [Im]. Ad; Wymondham, Norfolk.
Kb; The Champion Smokeless Cartridge.

T. L. HULL & CO. [Im]. Ad; 33 High St, Shaftesbury, Dorset.
Kb; The Shaston Special Smokeless.

HUNTER & SON (or SONS). [Gm]. Ad; 61-62 Royal Avenue, Belfast, Northern Ireland.
Kb; De Luxe, The Eclipse, Express Cartridge, The Favourite, The Ideal, The Invictus, The Long Shot, The Reliable (shown above), The Royal Cartridge, The Universal.

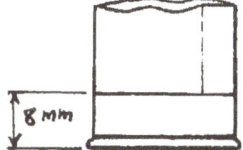 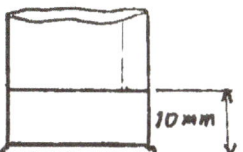 

WILLIAM HURLSTONE. [Im]. Ad; 50 Market Place, Warminster, Wilts.
Kb; Nk.
Rm; The above provisional drawings have been made from cartridge Remains. In one directory he was spelt as Hurlestone. Number 50 Market Place was renumbered as 49. He was not listed in an 1889 directory.

HENRY JOSEPH HUSSEY. Later as, H. J. HUSSEY LTD (Late of LANG & HUSSEY LTD). [Gm]. Ad; 81 New Bond St. Also at, 88 JERMYN ST, LONDON SW1.
Kb; Eley's Ejector, Joyce's Ejector, The Times.

HUTCHINSON. [Gm]. Ad; Kendal, Westmorland (Cumbria).
Kb; Nobel's Sporting Ballistite Special Cartridge.

IMPERIAL METAL INDUSTRIES (I.M.I.) LTD. ELEY AMMUNITION DIV.
Ad; Witton, Birmingham, Wes t Midlands.
Kb; 8 Gauge, 10 Gauge, 20 Gauge, Alphamax, Extra Long (410), Fourlong (410), Fourten, Gastight, Grand Prix, Grand Prix HV, Saluting Blank, Two-Inch, Winchester Cannon. Rm; This firm took over from the previous I.C.I. They Loaded for other firms. There were other brands that were crimp closed.

IRISH METAL INDUSTRIES LTD. [Ammunition Manufacturers].
Ad; 12 Dawson St, Dublin. Also at, Earles Island, Galway, Republic of Ireland.
Kb; Acme, Alphamax, Blackthorn Cartridge, Bonax, Nobel Clyde, Empire, Grand Prix, Klymax, Lia-Fail, Maximum, Mettax Cartridge, Noneka, Pegamoid, Primax, Special Trapshooting, Nobel's Sporting Ballistite, Westminster, Yeoman, Zenith.
Rm; This firm was started by the Eley-Kynoch Witton based firm in the late 1920's or early 1930's. The majority produced wer 12 gauge, a few 16 and 20 gauge were also produced. The firm was active until 1971.

IMPERIAL CHEMICAL INDUSTRIES (I.C.I.) METALS DIV (ELEY-KYNOCH) LTD. Ad, Offices, Millbank, London SW, Works, Witton, Birmingham, Warw (Midlands). Kb; 2" Deep Shell, 4, 8 and 10 Gauges, 20 Gauge Cartridge, 20 Gauge Case, 20th Century, 20th Century Deep Shell, Acme, Almac (brass 410), Alphamax, Alphamax High Velocity, Alphamax Neoflak, Big Bang (saluting), Blank, Blanks, Bonax, British Smokeless Cartridge (Also known as EDN eau-de-nil, British Smokeless Case (EDN), Buffalow, Bull's Eye, Cable Cutter (12g not shotgun), Coronation, Deep Shell, D.S.C, Ejector, Ejector Thin Brass, Empire, Empress, Extra Long (3" 410), Fourlong (410), Fourten , Gastight Quality Cartridge, Gastight Quality Case, G.P. (General Purpose, not Grand Prix), Grand Prix Cartridge, Grand Prix High Velocity, Grand Prix Case, Grand Prix Quality Case, Hollandia, Hymax, Impax, Juno, Maximum High Velocity, Maximum Neoflak, Mettax, Nitro Case, Nitron, Noneka, Parvo, Pegamoid Cartridge, Pegamoid Case, Practice Cartridge, Primax, Quail Smokeless, Red Flash Smokeless, Rocket, Saluting Blank, Saluting Blanks, Scarebird Cartridge, Smokeless Cartridge, Sporting Ballistite Cartridge, Sporting Ballistite Case, Trapshooting, Two-Inch, Universal (Kyblack), Unlined Nitro Case, Un Pinfire, Velocity, Westminster, Wildfowling, Winchester Cannon (starting Guns), Yeoman, Zenith. Rm; [Am,Cl, Wm]. Loaded for many other firms. Took over from Nobel Industries Ltd in 1926. Were taken over by I.M. I. Around 1962.

CHARLES INGRAM. [Gm]. Ad; 18 Renfield St. Later at, 4 Bothwell St. Still later at, 10 Waterloo St, Glasgow, Lanarks (Strathclyde).
Kb; The C. I., The Ingram, Special Loading, Un.
Rm; This firm had connection with the firm of , John D. Dougall & Sons.

INMAN MORROW & CO. [Gm]. Ad; 27 Queen Victoria St, Leeds, Yorks.
Kb; Un.

ALFRED JACKSON. {Im]. Ad; Abergavenny, Mon (Gwent).
Kb; Un.

H. G. JACKSON. [Gs, Im]. Ad; Bungay & Halesworth, Suffolk.
Kb; Un.

 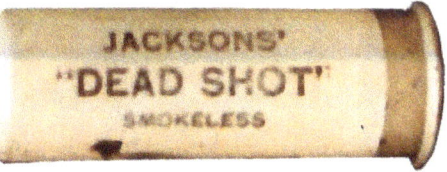 

WILLIAM JACKSON. Later as, JACKSON & SON. [Gm, Im].
Ad; 41 Silver St, Gainsborough, Lincs.
Kb; Best Gastight Woodcock Brand, Jackson's Dead Shot,
The Pheasant Loading.

JAMES & CO. [Millers, game food manufacturers and agricultural merchants].
Ad; Great Western Mills, Church St, Hungerford, Berks.
Kb; The Kennett Smokeless, Marlborough (shown above).
Rm; Closed down when their mills were gutted by fire after the second world war.

M. JAMES & SONS. [Im]. Ad; Newcastle Emlyn, Carmarthen (Dyfed).
Kb; The Gwalia

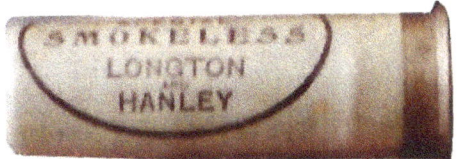 

JAMES & TATTON. [Im]. Ad; 14 Market St, Longton. Also at,
Hanley, Stoke-on-Trent, Staffs.
Kb; Special Smokeless.

A. R. & H. V. JEFFEREY LTD. [Gm]. Ad; 100 Old Town St, Plymouth, Devon.
Kb;410, The Eddystone, The Empire (shown above), The Empire Cartridge.

CHARLES JEFFERY. Later as, C. JEFFERY & SONS. [Gm].
Ad; 29 High St, Dorchester, Dorset.
Kb; The Ejector, The Empire, The Rabbit, The Royal Game, The Twenty.
Rm; Charles was known to have beeen active in 1898.

SAMUEL RICHARD JEFFERY. Later as, S. R. JEFFERY & SON LTD. [Gm].
Ad; 134 High St, Guildford, Surrey. Was at one time in Salisbury, Wilts.
Kb; Eley's Gas-tight Cartridge Case pinfire, 410 Long, 410 Short,
The Champion Smokeless (shown above), The Club, Smokeless Powder,
Special Smokeless.

WILLIAM JEFFERY & SON. [Gm]. Ad; 12 George St. Also at,
3 Russell St, Plymouth, Devon.
Kb; The Eddystone, The Flag, The Pegamoid, The Rabbit Special,
The Sky High (shown above), The Smeaton, Un.

W. J. JEFFERY & CO. Later, W. J. JEFFEREY & CO LTD. [Gm].
Ad; 13 King St, St James's. Also, 60 Queen Victoria St EC. Also, 26 Bury St, St James's. Finally, 9 Golden Square, Regent St, London W1.
Kb; The Champion, Club Smokeless, Ejector, High Velocity, The Jeffery Cartridge, Jeffery's XXX, Sharpshooter, Sharpshooters, The Vimite.

A.J. JEWSON. [Gm, Cl and sports outfitters].
Ad; 1 Westgate, Halifax, Yorks.
Kb, The Champion, The Crown, The Leader Cartridge, The Westgate, Un.

G. JOBSON.   Ad, Milford, Surrey.
Kb; The Milford Special Smokeless.

THOMAS JOHNSON & SON. [Gm, Cl]. Ad; Market Place, Swaffham, Norfolk.
Kb; The Reliable, Un.
Rm; Were known to have loaded pinfire cartridges.

JOHNSON & REID.   Ad; Darlington, Yorks (County Durham).
Kb; Eley's Gas-tight Cartridge Case (J & R's name on the stamping only).

JOHNSON & WRIGHT. [Iron merchants and Im].
Ad; 23A Gold St. Also at, Woolmonger St, Northampton, Northants.
Kb; The County, Kynock's Perfectly Gas-tight Case for E.C.
Rm; Know as active between 1894 and 1924.

HORATIO JONES. [Gm]. Ad; 25 High St, Wrexham, Denbighs (Clwyd).
Kb; Eley's Smokeless Cartridge (Jones name on the tube).
Rm; His business closed down in 1927.

W.P. JONES. Later as. W. PALMER JONES (GUNS) LTD. [Gm or Gs].
Ad; 25 Whittall St, Birmingham, Warw (W.Midlands).
Kb; The Accuratus, The Priority.
Rm; Estb 1826. Known as active in 1930's. Full name, William Palmer Jones.

Joyce's Ideal Smokeless Cartridge

FREDERICK JOYCE & CO LTD. [Am, Cl]. Ad; 57 Upper Thames St. Also at, 7 Suffolk Lane, London EC.
Kb; Bailey's Gastight Cartridge, The Bonnaud, Cannonite Powder, Ejector, Ejector Solid Drawn Case, F.J. Gastight, Ideal Smokeless, Improved Gastight for Amberite Smokeless, Improved Gastight for Schultze, Joyce's Gastight Cartridge Case for Walsrode, Improved Gastight for S.S., Improved Gastight for Walsrode, Joyce's D.B. Cartridge, Joyce's Long Brass, Joyce's National Cartridge Case, The National Smokeless Cartridge, Joyce's Royalty Cartridge, Special Nitro, Special Smokeless, The Waltham, Waterproof Gastight, Un.
Rm; As case manufacturers, numerous pin and centre fire were produced in many gauges. Apart from their own loading, many cases were sold in the UK and overseas to other firms that loaded their own. During 1907, the Nobel Explosives Company took over complete control of the Joyce plant for their own supply of cartridge cases.

H. JULIAN & SONS LTD. [Gs, Im]. Ad; 3-4 Church St, Basingstoke, Hants.
Kb; Eley's Gas-tight Cartridge Case for E.C. Powder (Julian's name on the stamping), Un (shown above).

 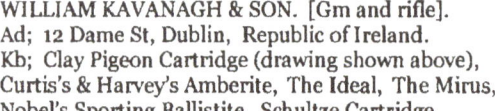 

WILLIAM KAVANAGH & SON. [Gm and rifle].
Ad; 12 Dame St, Dublin, Republic of Ireland.
Kb; Clay Pigeon Cartridge (drawing shown above),
Curtis's & Harvey's Amberite, The Ideal, The Mirus,
Nobel's Sporting Ballistite, Schultze Cartridge.

L. KEEGAN. [Gm or Gs]. Ad; 35 Upper Ormond Quay.
Also at, 3 Inns Quay, Dublin, Republic of Ireland.
Kb; The Bomb Shell (drawing shown above), The Emerald Isle,
The Faugh-A-Ballagh, The Lepracaun.

H. KEMPTON. Ad; Bloomfield Rd, Woolwich, London SE18.
Kb; Rottweil Express (Kempton's name on the over shot card).
Rm, Kempton used Rottweil cases. The distributor for Rottweil in the UK,
Leslie Hewett Ltd of Upton Cross, Liskeard, Cornwall.

 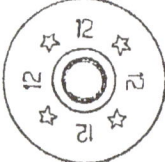 

KENT CARTRIDGE MANUFACTURING CO LTD. [Am].
Ad;; Branbridges Industrial Estate, East Peckham, Tonbridge, Kent.
Kb; Impact (shown above).
Rm; The majority of their brands are closed by a six fold crimp and
so they are not listed in this book.

ALFRED KENT. Later as KENT & SON. [Im, Gs, General furnishing and Coach hire, Cl]. Ad; Market Place, Wantage, Berks (Oxon).
Kb; Pinfire, Cheap Cartridge, Kynoch Perfectly Gas-tight EC powder, Kynoch Perfectly Gas-tight The Wantage, Gastight 410, The Wantage, Un.
Rm; Coach hire started after the first world war.

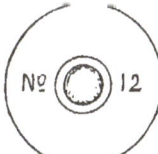

KENYON & TROTT. [plating business]. Ad; Cattle Market, Ipswich, Suffolk.
Kb;Un (shown above, name only on over shot card).

CHARLES KERR. [Gm]. Ad; 74 Hanover St, Stranraer, Wigtown (Dumfries & Galloway).
Kb; The Royal (shown above).

JOHN J. KILLEEN. Ad; Bridge House, Claremorris (Clar Chlainne Mhuiris), County Mayo, Republic of Ireland.
Kb; Fur & Feather (drawing shown above).

JAMES KIRK. [Gm]. Ad; 36 Union Buildings, Ayr, Ayrshire (Strathclyde).
Kb; Ayr Special, The Champion, Gastight Blue Roc Cartridge, The High Velocity, The Land of Burns, The Marksman, The Retriever, Special, Special Pegamoid, The Grouse.
Rm, This business incorporated in with Arthur Allan Ltd

KITHER. Ad; Seven Oaks, West Kent.
Kb; Eley's Gastight Cartridge Case for Schultze powder (drawing shown above, Kither's name on the over shot card only).

PETER KNIGHT. [Gm]. Ad; 39 Canal St (North). Later at, 22 Carrington St. Later still at, 12 Clinton St (East), Nottingham, Notts.
Kb; The Castle, The Invincibe, The Thurland.
Rm; The firm was known to have been active in 1881.

GEORGE KYNOCH. Later as G. KYNOCH & CO. Also as, KYNOCH LTD. [Am, Wm].
Ad; Cr 1874, 48 Hampton St, Birmingham. Also, 8 Cullum St, London EC. Cr 1862, Witton, Birmingham. Later to be, The Lion Works, Witton, Birmingham, Warwicks.
Kb Pinfire; Blue (first quality), Brown (good quality), Green (extra quality), Salmon (extra quality), Perfect (thin brass).
Kb Central fire; 410, 5/16" Brass, 5/8" Brass, Absolutteley Gastight Amberite Gunpowder, Amberite Smokeless, Beryl, Kynoch Big Bang, Blue (first quality), The Bonax, Brown (good quality), C.B. Cartridge Case, Deep-Head Gastight, Deep Shell, E.C. Gunpowder, Elax, Eureka (old Greek for I have found it), Gastigt Waterproof, Geranium Grouse, G.K. Special Smokeless, Green (extra quality), Haylex, The Kardax, The K.B. (Kynoch Black), The Kyblack, The Kynoid, Light Green Cartridge Case (Nitro powders), The Lion, Magic Shell (overseas market), Maroon Quality, The Nitro Ball, The Nitrone, The Opex, The Overlander (Australian Market), The Paradox Bullet Cartridge, Patent No 2090 Grouse Ejector, Patent Perfect Metalic, Perfectly Gastight, The Primax, The Quail Smokeless (overseas Markets), The Sallinoid (ball or bullet load), The Snipax, The Swift (sold in Australia), The Tellax (Cheap cartridge), Triumph Ballistite, Triumph Mullerite, Triumph Smokeless Diamond), Triumph Walsrode, Unlined Nitro Case, Use Berdan Primer, Warranted Gastight, Waterproof Case, The Witton, Witton Brand, Zulu.
Rm; Many of the above mentioned were made in various gauges. Also made Were 4 gauge and for punt guns and flare cartridges. Like it's competitors Elely Bros it marketed worldwide. It also loaded for other firms and sold ready Capped and printed cases. Some Gastights were spelt as Gas-tight. Cases were Spcially made for various gunpowders. Some of these were; Amberite, Cannonite, E.C., K.B. (Kynoch's Black), K.S.S. (Kynoch's Smokeless Sporting), Nonpriel, Normal, Schultze, Shotgun Rifleite, Sporting Ballistite, S.S., T.S. and Walsrode. This large firm was absorbed in to Explosives Trades Ltd, in Nov 1918. Many of their brand names were retained.

J. & H. LACEY. [Im]. Ad; Long Eaton, Derbys.
Kb; Imperial Special Smokeless (shown above).

T. LAMBERT LTD. [Gs, Im]. Ad; Parliament St, York, Yorks.
Kb; Lambert's Special Smokeless Cartridge.

CHARLES LANCASTER. Later as, C. LANCASTER & CO LTD. [Gm and cartridge developer].   For Ad, see Rm below.
Kb; Ejector, Generally Useful, The Leicester, Medium Game Cartridges, The Norfolk, Patent Gastight Cartridge, Lancaster's Pygmies, The Twelve-Twenty, Shoot Lancaster's Pygmies, Special Waterproof Cartridge.
Rm; The London Ad for Lancaster were as follows. 151 New Bond St, he was known to have been active here in 1889. At 11 Panton St, Haymarket, this Ad was circa 1925-32. Then my researched notes shown a return back to 151 New Bond St. This may not have been so as his firm may have owned both premises at the same time. Also I had made a note of him at being at, 2 Little Bruton St. These Ad can help in dating old cartridges. Lancaster & Co Ltd were finally incorporated into the London Gm, Grant & Lang. Also incorporated into Grant & Lang were the London Gm, Watson Bros.

 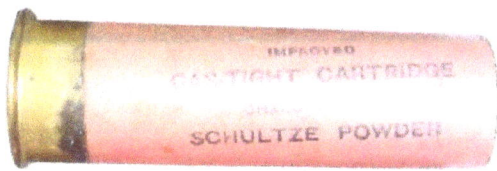

CHARLES E. LANE. [Im, universal provider]. Ad; Peterchurch, Golden Valley, Herefords (Hereford & Worcester).
Kb; Improved Gas-tight Cartridge Schultze Powder (shown above), Un.

CHARLES L. LANE. [Im]. Ad; 19-20 Cornhill, Bridgwater, Som.
Kb; Lane's Champion Smokeless Cartridge (shown above).
Rm; Directories listed them active between 1914 and 1923. They were not listed in the directories for 1919 and 1927.

JOSEPH H. LANG. Later as, J. LANG & SON. Later still as, J. LANG & SON LTD. [Gm, Cl]. Ad; 22 Cockspur St. Later at, 10 Pall Mall & 102 New Bond St, London W1.
Kb; 15 gauge pinfire, Kynoch Grouse Ejector, The Ventractor, Lang's Waterproof Pegamoid (shown above), Rm; Lang joined in with Stephen Grant in May 1925.

JOHN LANGDON. [Gs and cycle shop]. Ad; 20 St Mary St, Truro, Cornwall.
Kb; The Langdon (shown above).

JAMES JOHN LANGLEY. Later as, LANGLEY & LEWIS. [Gm, Cl].
Ad; Guildford St. Also at, 68 Bute St, & Park Square, Luton, Beds.
Was also in, Hitchin, Herts & Malden, Essex.
Kb; Blue Roc (shown above), British Smokeless, Grouse Ejector,
Prize Winner, The Severn, Un.

THOMAS LAW. Also, THOMAS LAW (JUNIOR). [Gm]. Ad; 17 King St,
Castle Douglas, Kirkudbright (Dumfries & Galloway).
Kb; Galloway Cartridge, Kynoch's Perfectly Gastight, Un.

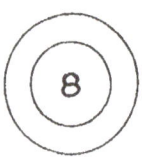  

LAWN & ALDER. [Colonial outfitters]. Ad; Brackley St, London EC.
Kb; L. & A. Half Brass, L. & A. Waterproof.

R. LEACH.   Ad; Oldham, Lancs (Great Manchester).
Kb; British Smokeless Case, Un (shown above).
Rm; The name, R. Leach, was on the over shot cards.

WILLIAM LEECH. Later as, W. LEECH & SONS. [Gm].
Ad; Conduit St, Chelmsford, Essex.
Kb; The Chelmsford Cartridge, The Club Smokeless, Essex County, Knoch's Grouse Ejector, Leech's Special Load, Pigeon Cartridge, Standard Cartridge, The X.L., Un.

HERBERT E. LEGGETT. [Im]. Ad; Broad St, Eye, Suffolk.
Kb; British Loaded Smokeless.

CHARLES LEONARD.   Ad; Market Place, Brigg, Lincs (Humberside).
Kb; The Glanford Cartridge.

LEWIS. [Im]. Ad; Wells, Somerset.
Kb; The Sunset.

 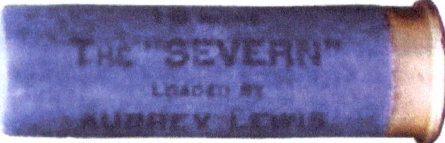 

AUBREY LEWIS. [Gm, Cl]. Ad; 19 Church St, Luton, Beds.
Kb; Blue Rock, The Chelt, Fourten, Eley G.P. (extra tube printing), High Velocity, The Severn (16 bore), The Special, Un.
Rm; Aubrey was once in partnership with James Langey. He continued gun making and finally closed his doors in 1969.

FRANK W. LIGHTWOOD. [Gs, Cl]. Ad; 122A Cleethorpe Rd. Later at, 172 Market Place, Brigg, Lincs (Humberside). Also at, 14 Market Place, Market Rasen, Lincs. Also in Grimsby, Lincs (Humberside).
Kb; The Four Best, Hy Vel Express, Lightwood, Woodcraft.

S. J. LIMMEX & Co.[Im, Gs].
2 High Street, Also Wood Street, Swindon, Wilts.
Cr; 1880 to end of 20th Centuary.
Nt; Remains found by metal detecting.

A. G. LINES & SONS. [Gun and ammunition dealers].
Ad; Stevenage, Herts.
Kb; The Super Shot, Un.

JAMES H. LININGTON. Ad; 107A St James's Square. Also at, 24 Union St, Newport, Isle of Wight. [Im, Gs].
Kb; Extra Special, Un pinfire.

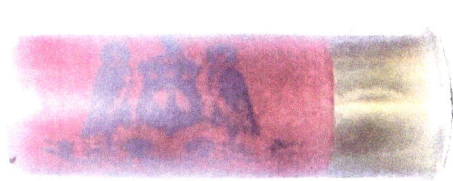 

 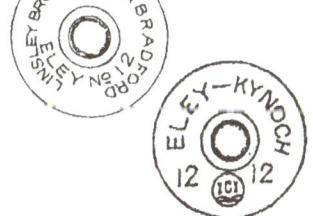

LINSLEY BROTHERS. [Gm]. Ad; Lands Lane. Also at, 97 Albion St. Also at, 137 Albion St, Leeds and also in Bradford, Yorks.
Kb; Eley Ejector, High Velocity, Kynoch Grouse Ejector, Nomis, Standard, Steel Lined Nitro, The Swift.
Rm; Established 1780.

ROBERT LISLE. [Gm]. Ad; Queen's Hall Buildings. Also at, 5 Arcade, Sadler Gate. Also at, 25 Derwent St, Derby, Derbys.
Kb; Lisle's Field Cartridge (one version shown above), Tiger Brand, The Victa Cartridge.

LLOYD & SONS. [Gm]. Ad; Station St, Lewes, Sussex.
Kb; Champion, Chanpion Ejector, County Cartridge, Imperial Crown, Improved Imps, Special, Special Imperial Champion, Standard.

LONDON SPORTING PARK LTD. Ad; 60 New Bond St, London W1.
Kb; Ejector (Their name on over shot card), Eley's Patent Gas-tight (name on over shot card, shown above), Eley Patent Gas-tight Case Pegamoid (their name on the stamping).

WILLIAM McCALL & CO. Later as, McCALL & SONS LTD. [Gm].
Ad; 23 Castle Street, Dumfries, Dumfries (Dumfries & Gallaway).
Kb; All British Popular Cartridge, Eley Bros EBL (McCall's name added), The Border Cartridge, K.C. (Keeper's cartridge), Tally Ho, The Signature.

McCRIRICK & SONS. [Gm]. Ad; 38 John Finnie St, Kilmarnock, Ayrs.
Kb; Ejector (name only on over shot card. Shown above), Un.

ALEX MACKAY & SON. {im]. Ad; Barmore St, Tarbert, West Loch, Argyll.
Kb; The Argyll (shown above).
Rm; Mackays started business in 1919 by taking over the Im business from John M. Macleod. John had fist started the business in 1874 when he purchased the Old Coaching Inn in Barmore St.

W. McMORRAN. Ad; Lanark, Lanarks (Strathclyde).
Kb; Special Smokeless.

JAMES MACNAUGHTON & SONS. [Gm]. Ad; Hanover St, Edinburgh, Midlothian. Also in Perth, Perths (Tayside).
Kb; Club Cartridge, Ejector, Eley Case (MacNaughton's name on brass stamping. Loaded with John's Patent Shrapnel Shell and shown above), Un.

JOHN MACPHERSON. Later as, J. MACPHERSON & SON. [Gm].
Ad; 24 Church St, Inverness, Inverness-shire (Highland).
Kb; The Bargate, Barrage Cartridge, The Clack, The Killer, The Royal (shown above), Un.

 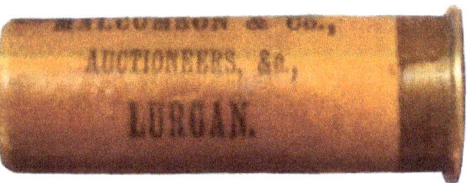 

J. MALCOMSON. Later as, J. MALCOMSON & CO. [Auctioneers].
Ad; Lurgan, Northern Ireland.
Kb; Un.

CHARLES HENRY MALEHAM. Later as, CHAS H. MALEHAM & CO. [Gm].
Ad; 5 West Bar, Sheffield, Yorks. Also at, 20 Regent St, London W1.
Kb; The Clay Bird, The Double Wing, The Field Cartridge, The Regent, The
Steeltown, The Wing Cartridge.   Rm; Chas was known as active circa 1914-18.
The Gm Arthur Turner took over the business in 1920.

MALLINSONS.   Ad; Great Driffield, Yorks (Humberside).
Kb; Mallinson's Shamrock Metal Lined, The Pheasant Cartridge.

PETER D. MALLOCH. [Gm or Gs]. Ad; 26 Scott St. Also, 34 Scott St, Perth,
Perthshire (Tayside).
Kb; The Matchless, The Red Grouse, The Standard, The Triumph (shown above).

ALLAN MANBY. [Im]. Ad; 69 High St, Southwold, Suffolk.
Kb; The Suffolk Champion.

F. MANBY & BROTHER. [Im]. Ad; 62 High St, Skipton, Yorks.
Kb; Manby's Special (shown above).

MANTON & CO. [Gm and rifle]. Ad; Calcutta & NewDelhi, India.
Also a London office, Ad not known.
Kb; Manton's Contractile, Manton's Express Cartridge, Manton's For India, Manton's Special, Standard Smokeless, Manton's Tiger Brand Cartridge (shown above), Un.   Rm; Shown here, as a London Ad.

MARSHALL & PEARSON.   Ad; Fort-William, Inverness-shire (Highland).
Kb;The Lochaber Cartridge (shown above).

A. H. MARTIN.   Ad; Cross Ash, Abergavenny, Mon (Gwent).
Kb; Trent Best Smokeless (extra tube printing).

ALEX MARTIN LTD. [Gm]. Ad; 20 Royal Exchange Square, Glasgow. Also at, 25 Bridge St, and 128 Union St, Aberdeen, Aberdeens (Grampian). Also at, 18 Frederick St, Edinburgh, Midlothian. Were also at, Friar St, Stirling, Stirlings. Kb; The Age, The Calendonia, The Club, Eley Case, Hand Loaded, High Velocity, The Scotia, The Stirling, The Thistle, Thistle High Velocity, The Velm, Un.

J. F. MASON. [Country gent]. Ad; Eynsham Hall, Eynsham, Oxon.
Kb; Eley's Ejector [Pc] (Mason's name on stamping, shown above).

 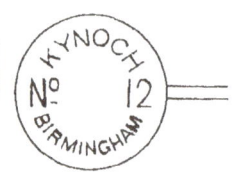

W. MELLARD. {Im}. Ad; Denbigh, Denbighshire (Clwyd).
Kb; Un (pinfire 12 gauge).

H. L. MEREDITH. [Im].
Ad; 18 High St, Bideford, Devon.
Kb; Meridith's Special.

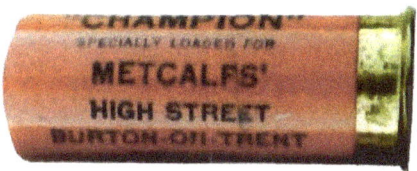 

G. F. METCALF.   Ad; 90 High St, Burton-on-Trent, Staffs.
Kb; The Champion.

R. METCALFE. [Gm]. Ad; 5 Market Place, Richmond, Yorks.
Kb; The Richmond, The Swaledale, Special Smokeless.

W. METCALFE. [Gm or Gs]. Ad; 5 Market Place, Richmond. Also at, Shute Red, Catterick Camp, Yorks.
Kb; Metcalfe's Special, Un (shown above).
Rm; W. Metcalfe followed on from Robert Metcalfe at the same address. They are shown here separate because of additional Ad and changed cartridge names.

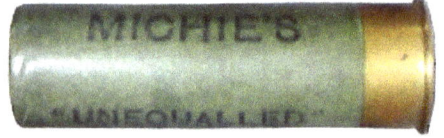 

G . M. MICHIE & CO.   Ad; Stirling, Stirlings (Grampian).
Kb; Michie's Unequalled shown above).
Rm; All cartridges marked, 'Michie Stirling' are pre 1894.

 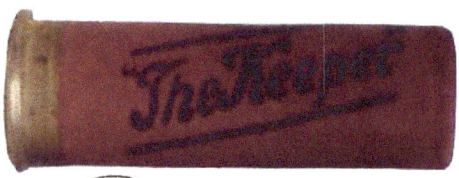

MIDLAND GUN CO. [Gm, Cl]. Ad; Gun Works, Bath St, Birmingham, Warw (W. Midlands). Also at, Brigg, Lincs (Humberside).
Kb; 410 Long, 410 Short, Best of All, Demon Cartridge, Demon Waterproof, The Double Demon, The Edward, Ejector, Gastight Steel Lined, The Imp, The Jubilee, The Keeper, The Keeper High Velocity, Perfect Smokeless, The Perfection, The Perfection Smokeless, Pewitt (light load), The Rabbit Smokeless Cartridge, The Rabbit Special Smokeless, The Record, Smokeless Gastight Cartridge, Smokeless Hand Loaded, Special Smokeless Cartridge, Sudden Death, Un.

W. MILBURN. Later as, MILBURN & SON. [Gs, Cl]. Ad; 5-7 High Cross St, Brampton, Cumberland (Cumbria).
Kb; The Don, Kynoch's Grouse Ejector, The Milburn, M.S.B. (Milburn & Son Brampton), The Noxall, The Rex, Special Loading, Un.   Rm; Established 1776.

R. MILLETT.   Ad; Ilminster, Som.
Kb; Eley Deep Shell Case (Millett's name only on over shot card).

MODERN ARMS CO LTD. [Ammunition dealers]. Ad; 58 Southwark Ridge Rd, London SE1.
Kb; Star Standard Special Smokeless (410 shown above).
Rm; Not known if they had their name printed on a cartridge. The above were also marketed in gauges, 12, 16, 20 and 28.

B. D. MOGG & SON.   Ad; Wells, Somerset.
Kb; The Mendip (shown above).

W. H. MOHK. Also known as, HENRY MONK. [Gm].
Ad; 77 Foregate St, Chester, Cheshire.
Kb; The Imperial, Pegamoid, The Popular, The Royal,
The Straight, Un. Rm; Many Un were in 12,16 and 20g.

CHARLES MOODY. Later became, W.F. MOODY. [Gm and cutler].
Ad; 13 Church St, Romsey, Hants.
Kb; Kynoch Perfectly Gas-tight (Moody's name only on top card), The Ranger Special Smokeless, Waterproof Non Corrosive, Un, (blue quality).
Rm; Charles was known to have been active in 1901.

W. F. MOODY. [Gm, cutler]. Ad; 13 Church St, Romsey, Hants.
Kb; The Ranger Special Smokeless, Moody's Special Waterproof Non Corrosive (shown above).
Rm; W. F. Followed on after Charles in Romsey.

THOMAS HENRY MOOR.   Ad; 23 Broad St, South Molton, Devon.
Also at, Exford, Somerset.
Kb; The Molton, The Molton Special, The Rabbit, Special Rabbit Cartridge.

FRED T. MORGAN. [Gs, Im]. Ad; Talgarth, Brecon (Powys).
Kb; The Red Dragon.

 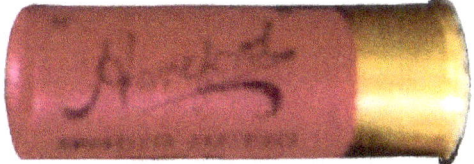 

P. MORRIS & SON. [Gs, Im]. Ad; 4 High St, Hereford, Herefs (H & W).
Kb; Hereford, The Imperial, The Lightning Cartridge.

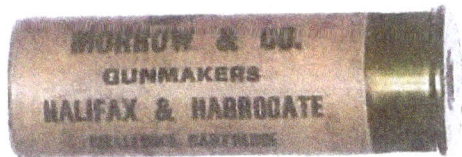

MORROW & CO. (W. R. WEDGWOOD). [Gm]. Ad; 4 Horton st, Halifax.
Also at Harrowgate, Yorks.
Kb; The Challenge Cartridge.

MORTIMER. Later as, MORTIMER & SON. [Gm]. Ad; 86 George St,
Edinburgh, Midlothian.
Kb; Eley's Patent Gas-tight Cartridge Case, Un.   Rm; Incorporated the
Business of Joseph Harkom & Sons Ltd. Then in 1938 they themselves
Were incorporated into John Dickson & Son Ltd.

MULLERITE CARTRIDGE WORKS. Also known as, BRITISH MULLERITE (Proprietor MARTIN PULVERMANN & CO LTD). [Cl and merchants].
Ad; 59 Bath St. Also at, St Mary's Row, Birmingham, Warw (W. Midlands).
Kb; The Ace, The Ace Long Range, The Black Prince, The British Champion, The Champion Smokeless, The Champion Smokeless Heavy Load, Fourtenner Long, Fourtenner Short, General Service Cartridge (shown above), Green Seal, Grey Seal, Heyman Smokeless, Metalode, Red Seal, Silver Ray, Smokeless, Special Clayking, Yellow Seal, Un.
Rm; Some of the above named may have been loaded for other firms. Not all of these Mullerite loaded cartridges carried the Mullerite name. Note the monogram standing for Martin Pulvermann & Co Ltd.

R. C. MUMFORD. Ad; 66 High St, Southwold, Suffolk.
Kb; The Stopper.

T. W. MURRAY & CO LTD. [Gm and fishing tackle makers]. Ad; The Munster Armoury, 87 Patrick St, Cork, County Cork, Republic of Ireland.
Kb; Kynoch Extra Quality Cartridge Case, Murray's Reliable (also known as The TWM), The Munster Speedwell, The Special Cartridge, Special Loading, The Speedwell Smokeless, The Wildfowler.

NATIONAL ARMS & AMMUNITION Co. Often shown as, N. A. & A. CO.
Ad; Perry Bar, Birmingham, Warw (West Midlands).
Kb; Ejector, Express, Un.
Rm; They were active circa 1872-1882. They sold thin walled one piece brass cases. These have been seen in 14 and 16 gauge.

J. V. NEEDHAM. [Gm]. Ad; 20A Temple St. Also at, Damascus Works, Loveday St, Birmingham, Warw (W. Midlands).
Kb; Shoot Needham's guns and Cartridges, Uneedem Smokeless Cartridges (shown above).

FRANCIS NELSON. Later as, F. NELSON & SONS LTD.
Ad; Sligo, County Sligo, Republic of Ireland.
Kb; The Favourite, The Reliable (shown above).

A. NESTOR. Later as NESTOR BROS.   Ad; 28 O'Conner St, Limerick, Republic of Ireland.
Kb; The Shannon, Un (Their name on the stamping. Shown above).

NEWLAND & STIDOLPH [Im]. Ad; Stratford-upon-Avon, Warw. Un;

GEORGE NEWNHAM. Later as, NEWNHAM & CO. [Gm].
Ad; 29 Comercial Rd, Landport. Also at, 8 Queens Rd, Buckland, Portsmouth, Hants.
Kb; The Champion, The Keepers Cartridge, Kynoch's Deep Shell Cartridge Case, The Special Game (shown above).

 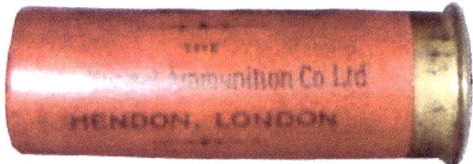 

NEW NORMAL AMMUNITION CO LTD. [Cl]. Ad; Clutterhouse Lane. Also at, 37 John's Avenue, Church End, Hendon, London NW4.
Kb; Gastight, The Hendon, The New Normal Ammunition Co, The Nimrod, The Normalis, Special Twenty.   Rm; Their Ad in 1911-12 was Clutterhouse Lane. Later to be Clutterhouse Rd. They were listed 1926-1939 at 37 John's Avenue.

 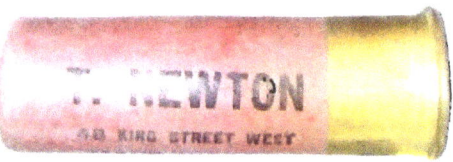 

T. NEWTON. [Gm]. Ad; 48 King St (West), Manchester, Lancs (Great Manchester).
Kb; The Lightning, Eley's Gas-tight Cartridge Case for Schultze Gunpowder, Newton's G.P., Pegamoid Brand Paper, The Smokeless Cartridge, Un.

THE NEW EXPLOSIVES CO LTD. [Am, Pm]. Ad; 62 London Wall, London EC2. Works and Mills at, Stowmarket, Suffolk.
Kb; Felixite, Fourten, The Go Lightly Cartridge, The Green Rival, The Neco, The N.E. Powder, The Premier (Neonite), The Primrose Smokeless, The Red Rival, Red Star Smokeless Powder, Sixteen Bore, Twenty Bore, Un.
Rm; Many brands were named from the powders used. Not all, but most cases were from Messrs Eley Bros. They were active loading between 1907-1920. See also the E.C. Powder Co Ltd in this book.

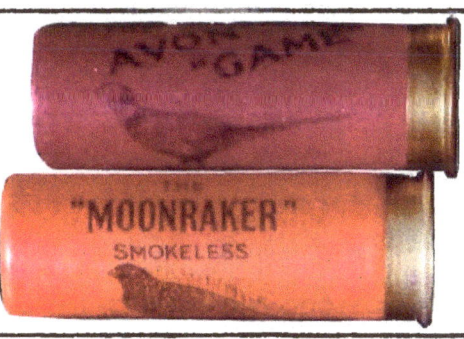

A.P. NIGHTINGALE & SON LTD' [Im, Id]. Ad; 47 Canal, Salisbury, Wilts. Kb; The Avon, Avon Game, The Moonraker Smokeless.
Rm; Shown as Im in a 1903 Directory but not shown as Im in 1907 directory. It had gone Id. Know to have had Frank Dyke Loadings.

NITROKOL POWDER CO.   Ad; London. (Rest of Ad is not known).
Kb; The Redskin, The Rover (shown above).

NOBEL EXPLOSIVES CO LTD. [Am, Pm]. Ad; 149 & 195 West George St, Glasgow, Lanarks (Strathclyde). Also at, College Hall Chambers, Cannon St. And also at, 1 Arundel St, The Strand, London WC. Their first factory was at, Ardeer on the banks of the Garnock, Ayrshire. Their second factory was built at, Waltham, Essex.

Kb 1; 'A' Cartridge Case, Ajax, Bar Won, Challenge, Clyde, Deep Shell, Derwent, Ejector, Empire, Gas-tight Waterproof Cartridge Case, Gas-tight Waterproof Cartridge Case UL (unlined), Grampian, Kardax, Kingsway, National, New Era, Nile, Nitro Cartridge Case, Noneka, Orion, Parvo, Perfect, Pegamoid, Primrose Ballistite, Regent, Special Primrose, Smokeless Ballistite Smokeless Special Cartridge, Target, Unitro Cartridge Case, Un.

Kb 2; Thought to have been for Australian and other overseas markets;
Corio, Coronet, Don Smokeless, Emerite Smokeless, Excelsior, Fox, Gas-tight Waterproof Belloid Paper, Red Indian, Rex, Ringer, Starling, Sun.

Rm; Founded in 1871 as, The British Dynamite Co. Several cartridge brand names are of their powder names. In 1907, Nobel's took over the controlling interest of, F. Joyce & Co Ltd for their own cartridge cases. In November 1918 the firm merged into a large new firm. See the next entry.

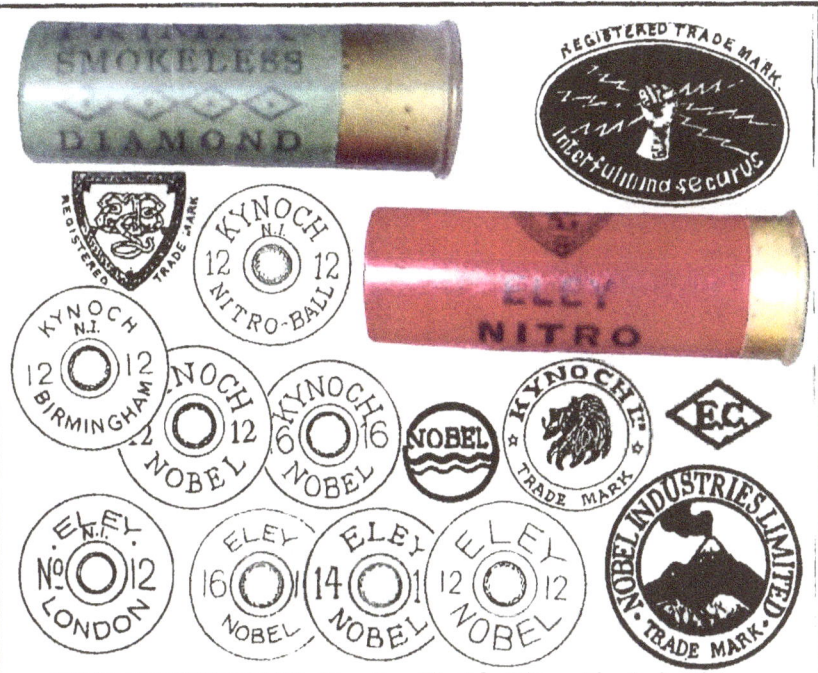

NOBEL INDUSTRIES LTD. [Am, Pm, Cl]. Ad; Witton, Birmingham' Warw (W.Midlands).
Kb; Acme, Albion, Amberite, Bonax, British Smokeless, Clyde, Deep Shell, Deep Shell Case, Ejector, Eley Extra Long (410), Fourlong, Fourten, Gastight, Gastight Quality Case, Grand Prix, Grand Prix Quality Case, Hollandia, Juno, Kardax, Lethal Ball, Magic Shell, Majestic, Nitro Case, Nitrone, Parvo, Pegamoid, Primax, Smokeless Cartridge, Standard Unlined, Sure Shot (South African market), Trapshooting, Twenty Gauge, Two-Inch, Velocity, Westminster, Winchester Cannon, Yeoman, Zenith, Kynoch 5/16" Brass, Kynoch 5/8" Brass, Pinfire, Un.
Rm; Continued as N.I. until circa 1926 when I.C.I. took over the controlling interests as, I.C.I. Metals Division (Eley-Kynoch) Ltd.

SYDNEY A. NOBBS. [Im, taxidermist and fishing tackle dealer].
Ad; 2 Norman St, Lincoln, Lincs.
Kb; The Sureshot (Nobb's name on tube and loaded by Jas R. Watson & Co. Shown above).

NORMAL POWDER CO. Later as, NORMAL POWDER & AMMUNITION CO LTD. [Cl, Pm]. Ad; 2 Bank Buildings, Cricklewood. Also in Hendon, London W4.
Kb; Hendon (shown above), Un.   Rm; Possibly may have used names that are listed in the Normal Improved Ammunition Co. Could have had U.S.A. connections.

B. NORMAN. Later as, NORMAN & SONS. [Gm]. Ad; Woodbridge & Framlinham, Suffolk.
Kb; The Gastight, The Service, The Special, The Standard.
Rm; Established 1870.

C. W. Norton. [Im]. Ad; Newton, Mont (Powys).
Kb; Un.

JAMES ODELL. [Im]. Ad; 62 High St, Stony Stratford, Bucks.
Kb; Smokeless Cartridge (shown above).

OLBYS LTD.   Ad; Ashford, Canterbury, Folkstone, Margate & Ramsgate, Kent.
Kb; Olbys Cantium (shown above).

O'RIORDAN & FORREST.
Ad; Midleton, County Cork, Republic of Ireland.
Kb; Un.

C. PARSONS. Later as, PARSONS SHERWIN & CO LTD. [Id].
Ad; Nuneaton & Coventry, Warw (W. Midlands).
Kb; Special Loading, Un.

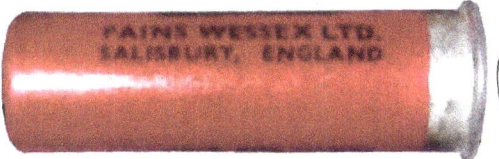 

JAMES PAIN & SONS. Later as, PAINS WESSEX LTD. [Pyrotechnics and signal Cartridge manufacturers]. Ad; Salisbury, Wilts. Also at, Mitcham, London.
Kb; Bird Scaring Cartridge (not for shotgun), Ejector.

A. PAGE WOOD. [Gm]. Ad; Baldwin St, Bristol, Glos (Avon).
Also, PAGE WOOD & CO. [Gm]. Ad; 39-40 Walcot St, Bath, Som (Avon).
Kb; I Defy All To Approach it Lion Brand Unapproachable , Un (name only on stamping and shown above).
Rm; This firm was not sure as what to call itself in its infancy. Thanks to Mrs M. Joyce, librarian, I have the following taken from Bath directories. 1890-91 under the Gm title, Wood Page & Co at 39 -40 Walcot St. While listed under Walcot St, Wood Alfred gun manufacturers. There was no mention of Page. Directories 1892-93 the firm was listed as, Wood Page & Co., and then T. Page Wood & Co. Prior to 1890 and after 1893, no more listings of this firm although 40 Walcot St was occupied either side. This then dates the illustrated above To circa 1892.

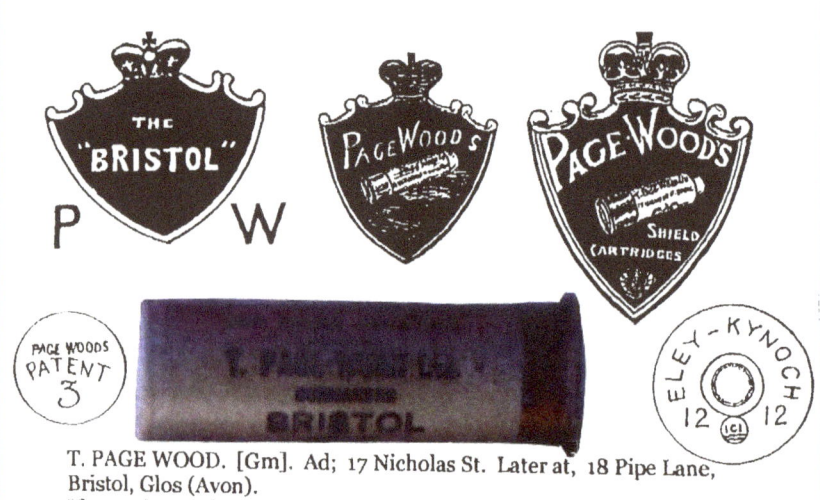

T. PAGE WOOD. [Gm]. Ad; 17 Nicholas St. Later at, 18 Pipe Lane, Bristol, Glos (Avon).
Kb; Anti-Recoil Cartridge, Anti-Recoil Economic Cartridge, The Bristol, The Climax Cartridge (shown above), The Double Crimp, First Quality, The Imperial Crown, The National Choke Cartridge, The Page-Wood No 2, The Page-Wood D.S., The Page-Wood's Shield Cartridge, The Park Row, Second Quality, Special 410, The Wildfowler.

 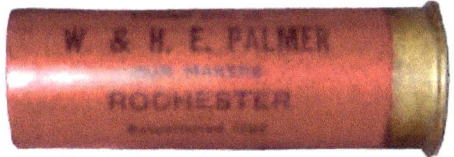 

W. & H. E. PALMER. [Gm]. Ad; 85 High St, Rochester, Kent.
Kb; The Century, Un.

 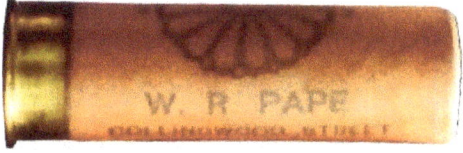 

WILLIAM ROCHESTER PAPE. [Gm]. Ad; 21 Collingwood St, Newcastle-upon-Tyne, Nthmb. Also at, Sunderland, County Durhan (Tyne & Wear).
Kb; The Beryl, The Heather, The Pointer, The Ranger Smokeless, The Setter, The Tyne, Pinfire, Un.   Rm; William produced many cartridges without brand names. One illustrated a picture of his gun shop and works on the tube.

TOM PARKINSON.   Ad; Ulverston, Lancs (Cumbria).
Kb; Un.

 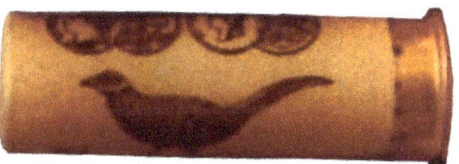 

JOHN PATSTONE & SON. [Gm]. Ad; 25 High St. Later at 28 High St, Southampton, Hants. Were at one time in Winchester, Hants.
Kb; The Precision, The Reliable, The Renown, Un.
Rm; Clarke, Cox, Macpherson and Patstone seem to have a tangled history in Salisbury and Southampton. I do not know their full histories.

PATSTONE & COX. [Gm]. Ad; 28 High St, Southampton, Hants.
Was also at one time in, Winchester, Hants.
Kb; The Pheasant (shown above), The Pheasant Cartridges,
The Precision.

J. C. PATTERSON. [Im]. Ad; The Corner House, Market Square,
Lisburn, Northern Ireland.
Kb; The Nailer Smokeless Cartridge.

JOSEPH PEACE LTD. [Gm and sports outfitter].
Ad; Darlington, County Durham.
Kb; Eley G.P. Case, Un.
Rm; Peace's name was seen on the over shot cards.

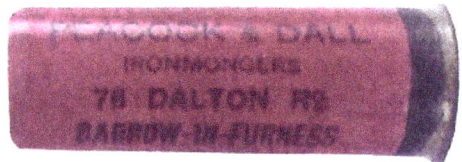

PEACOCK & DALL. [Im]. Ad; 76 Dalton Rd, Barrow-in-Furness, Lancs (Cumbria).
Kb; Un.

PEARSON & CO.   Ad; Grimsby, Lincs (Humberside).
Kb; Nobel's Sporting Ballistite (Pearson's name on the tube printing).

 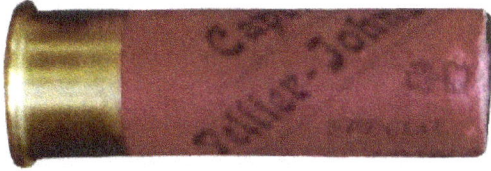

CAPTAIN E. PELLIER-JOHNSON.   Ad is not known.
Kb; Special loading by Eley Bros Ltd (shown above).
Rm; A private cartridge.

 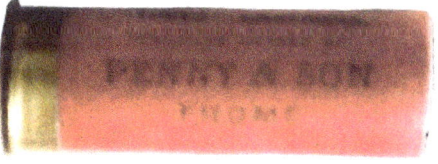 

PENNY & SON.   Ad; Frome, Somerset.
Kb; The Times Cartridge.

PHILLIP BROS. [Im]. Ad; 141 High St, Marlborough, Wilts.
Kb; No known cartridge.
The provisional drawing was made from metal detected remains.

PHILLIPS & POWIS. [Cycle motorcar and aviation agents].
Ad; 34 & 37 West St, Reading, Berks.
Kb; The Pheasant (drawing shown above).
Rm; In later years they went into business with Miles Aircraft at Woodley.

THE PHEASANT

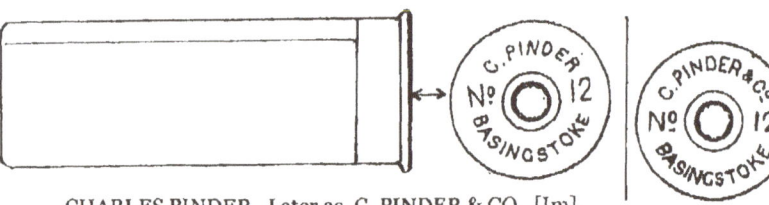

CHARLES PINDER. Later as, C. PINDER & CO. [Im].
Ad; Market Place, Basingstoke, Hants.
Rm; No known cartridge. The provisional drawing was made from metal detected remains. He was known as active in 1911.

J.E.PINDER. [Im]. Ad; 1 Winchester St Corner, Market Place, Salisbury, Wilts. [Im].
Kb; Pinder's Dead Shot Smokeless.
Rm; Not listed in a 1907 directory, but was listed in a 1920 directory. They were Known active by the start of the second world war. At least one brand was loaded By Frank Dyke.

PINK.   Ad;Romford & Barking, Essex.
Kb; Demon Smokeless Cartridge.

HERBERT B. PITT. [Im]. Ad; 7 Silver St. Also at, 37 Roundstone St, Trowbridge, Wilts.
Kb; H.B. Pitt's Premier (shown above).
Rm; He was not listed in an 1899 directory. He was listed as active in 1903. In 1920 he still had 7 Silver St, and was still there in 1939.

 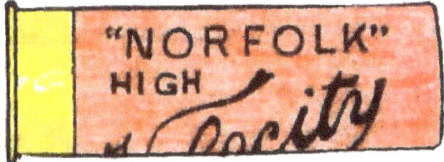

S. PLUMBERS LTD. [Gun and ammunition dealers].
Ad; Great Yarmouth, Norfolk.
Kb; Norfolk High Velocity Load (drawing shown above), The Original Norfolk.

PNEUMATIC CARTRIDGE CO LTD. [Cl]. Ad; 61-67 Albert St. Also at, 96-98 Holyrood Rd, Edinborough, Midlothian.
Kb; Ejector, Pneuma, Pneumatic No 1, Pneumatic No 2, Pneumatic No 3, Pneumatic 410, Pneumatic Cartridge, Pneumatic Trapshooting Cartridge, Pneumatic Twenty Gauge. Rm; Later made a move to Bristol.

 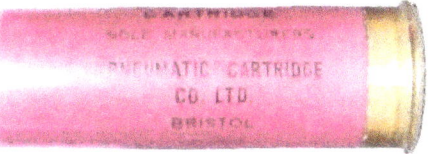 

PNEUMATIC CARTRIDGE CO LTD. [Cl]. Ad; Bristol, Glos (Avon).
Kb; Pneumatic Cartridge.
Rm; Were active at Bristol circa, 1954-1968.

HERBERT EDWARD POLLARD & CO. [Gm]. Ad; 62 Broad St, Worcester, Worcs (H & W. Hereford & Worcester).
Kb; Gas-tight, The Keepers Smokeless, The Long Shot, Our Game, Un.

POND & SON. [Im, agricultural merchants].
Ad; Market Place, Blandford Forum, Dorset.
Kb; Un pinfire (drawing shown above).
Rm; Their telephone number was, Blandford 1.

S. E. PORTER & CO.   Ad; 16-18-20 High St, Whitchurch, Salop.
Kb; Gyttorp (Porter's name on the top card only, Un.

J. Y. POTTER.   Ad; King's Lynn, Notfolk.
Kb; Eley's Gas-tight Cartridge Case for E.C. Powder (Name only on the over shot card, shown above).

 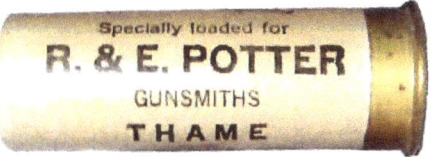 

ROBERT & ERNEST POTTER. [Gs, Im]. Ad; 3 High St, Thame, Oxon.
Kb; Un (shown above).

WILLIAM POWELL & SON (GUNMAKERS) LTD. [Gm].
Ad; 35 Carrs Lane, Birmingham, Warw (West Midlands).
Kb; Admiral, Clay Bird, Curtis's & Harvey's Smokeless Diamond, Gastight Metal Lined, General, Knockout, Kynoch's Ejector, Marshal, Pegamoid, Powell's Ejector, Specially Hand Loaded, The Steel Lined, Super Velocity.

W. J. POWELL. [Gm]. Ad; Leiston, Suffolk.
Kb; The Lightning Smokeless (shown above).

PROGRESSIVE CARTRIDGE CO.   Ad; Chandlersford, Hants.
Kb; Un (drawing shown above).

C. F. PUGH. [Im]. Ad; Knighton, Radnorshire (Powys).
Kb; The Rabbit.

ARTHUR F. PUNTER. Later as, A.F. PUNTER Proprietor J.M. EMBERTON. [Im].
Ad; 46 Wote St, Basingstoke, Hants.
Kb; The Minimax, F.D. Shamrock, The Farmer's Friend (F.D loading).
Rm; Estb 1904. Catalogue illustrated a Punter cartridge with a cock pheasant.

C. PURCELL.
Ad; 10 Worcester St, Gloucester, Glos.
Kb; Special High Velocity Cartridge (shown above).

JAMES PURDEY. Later as, J. PURDEY & SON LTD. Still later,
J. PURDEY & SONS LTD. [Gm, Cl]. Ad; 57-60 Audley House, Audley St,
London W1.
Kb; 2-Inch, Eley's Ejector, Pegamoid, Purdey's Deep Shell, Purdey's
Large Cap, Purdey's Special, Pinfire, Un. Rm; Loaded for British Royalty.

R. S. PURDEY. [Im, Cl]. Ad; Thirsk, Yorks.
Kb; Warranted Gas-tight Cartridge Case (shown above).
Rm; The above was loaded with a John's Patent Shell. An old cartridge box with Pudey's name was made by, W.A. Stubbs of Corbridge, Staffs.

PURVIS & CO.   Ad; Alnwick, Northumberland.
Kb; Sure Shot.

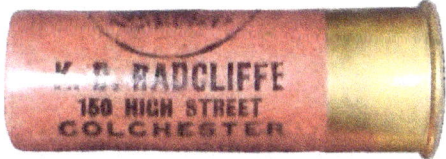

K. D. RADCLIFFE. [Gm or Gs]. Ad; 150 High St, Colchester, Essex.
Kb; A True Fit, Warranted Gastight (shown above), Un.
Rm; Radcliffe took over from J. S. Boreham in November 1899. Note that all cartridges by J. S. Boreham belong to the 19th Centuary.

ROBERT RAINE. Later as, RAINE BROTHERS. [Gm].
Ad; Carlisle, Cumberland (Cumbria).
Kb; The Border Cartridge, The Irresistible, Raine's Special.

F. RANDELL LTD. [Im]. Ad; Market Place, North Walsham.
Also at, Cromer, Norfolk.
Kb; Special Smokeless (shown above).

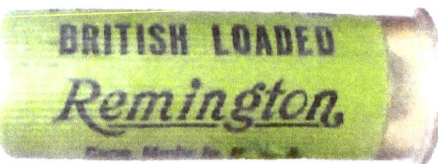  

REMINGTON ARMS, UNION METALIC CARTRIDGE CO LTD. Also known as, REMINGTON U.M.C. (ENGLAND). [Am, Cl, Wm]. Ad; Offices at, Bush House, Aldwych, London WC2. Factory at, UMC Works, Brimsdown, Enfield, Middx. Kb; Arrow, Economy, Remington 410, Kleanbore, Nitro Club, Remilion Geranium. Rm; Know active in 1913. Loaded U.S.A. cases and also for other firms.

E.G.E. REYNOLDS. [Sports depot]. Ad; Saxmundham, Suffolk.
Kb; The Champion Smokeless.

REYNOLDS & WADSWORTH. Ad; Barnsley, Yorks. [Gm].
Kb, Eley Bros Gastight.

RHODES & PAGET. [Im]. Ad; Cook Lane, Keighley, Yorks.
Kb; Un.
Rm; Firms names on over-shot wads. Known active in 1913. Unfortunately No other directories available, but not listed in 1936.

C. C. RICHARDS. [Im]. Ad; Wiveliscombe, Somerset.
Kb; The Wivey Special Smokeless (shown above).

 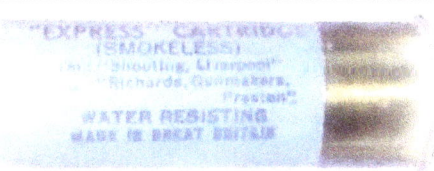 

WILLIAM RICHARDS. Later as, W. RICHARDS (LIVERPOOL) LTD. [Gm].
Ad; 27 Old Hall St, Liverpool, Lancs (Merseyside). Also at, 44 Fisher Gate, Preston, Lancs.
Kb; The Castle, The Express, Grand Prix, The Killwell, Kynoch's Grouse Ejector, The Mark Down, The R. P. Cartridge, The R.P. Gastight Smokeless Cartridge.

G. M. RICHARDSON.
Ad; Dumfries, Dumfries-shire (Dumfries & Galloway).
Kb; Buccleuch (shown above), Criffel, Ideal.

 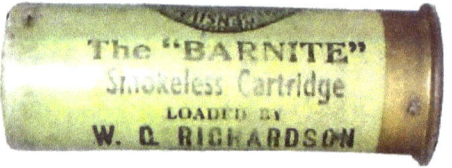 

WILLIAM G. RICHARDSON LTD. [Cartridge and fishing tackle experts].
Ad; Barnard Castle, County Durham.
Kb; The Baliol, The Barnite (shown above), The Barnoid, Nulli Secundus.

JOHN RIGBY. Later as, J. RIGBY & CO (GUNMAKERS) LTD. [Gm and rifle].
Ad; 24 Suffolk St, Dublin, Republic of Ireland. Also at, 72 St James's St. Later
At, 43 Sackville St. Later still at, 32 King St, St James's, London SW1.
Kb; Ejector, Rigby's Record Cartridge, Un.   Founded in Dublin in 1770
a centurary before breech loading. Were in Sackville St, in 1927.

C. RIGGS & CO LTD. [Gm or Gs]. Ad; Ye Bishop's Gate Sports House,
107 Bishopgate, London EC.
Kb; The Bishop, The Gate (shown above), The Mitre.

A. E. RINGWOOD. [Gm]. Ad; Banbury, Oxon.
Kb; The Dreadnought, The Ideal, The Special, Un.

AUGUSTUS J. ROBERTS. [lm]. Ad; 55 Broad St, Ludlow, Salop.
Kb; The Roberts Special Smokeless.

H. ROBINSON.   Ad; 102 St John's St, Bridlington Yorks.
Kb; The Burlington Express (shown above).

ROBERT ROBINSON. Later as, R. ROBINSON (GUNMAKERS) LTD. [Gm].
Ad; 7 Queen St, Kingston-upon-Hull, Yorks (Humberside).
Kb; The Champion, Ejector, The Humber, The Kingston Smokeless,
The Magnet, Sporting Ballistite, Un.
Rm; Robinson was taken over by Joe Wheater post World War Two.

R. B. RODDA & CO. [Dealers in guns and ammunition].
Ad; Callcutta, India. Also in, Birmingham, Warw (W. Midlands), UK.
Kb; 3 inch Long Range, Champion Smokeless, Crown Smokeless,
Mullerite Paragon, Rotax Ball, The Wellesley (shown above).
Rm; This firm had stronger connections with India than in the UK.

S. J. ROGERS.   Ad; Baddesley, Southampton, Hants.
Kb; Un (shown above, name only on over shot card).

CHARLES ROSSON. Later as, ROSSON & CO. [Gm]. Ad; 4 Market Head, Derby, Derbys. Rm, Later the firm moved to Norwich as,
C. S. ROSSON & CO LTD. [Gm, Cl]. Ad; 13 Rampant Horse St. Later at, Bedford St, Norwich, Norfolk.
Kb; C.R. Black Powder, The Crown, The Eclipse, Ejector, The Ektor Long 410, The Kuvert, The Lowrecoil, The Monvill, Pegamoid, Pigeon, The Roedich, The Sixteen Cartridge, Smokeless, Star 410, The Twenty Cartridge, The Vipax, The Waveney, Un.

B. L. ROSKELLEY. [Im, optician and diamond merchant].
Ad; 20 Queen St, Lostwithiel, Near St Austell, Cornwall.
Kb; Un.
Rm; The above provisional drawing has been made from metal Detected remains.

R. H. ROWLAND. [Im]. Ad; Thoroughfare, Woodbridge, Suffolk.
Kb; Special Loading.

JOHN ROWLATT. [Gm or Gs]. Ad; 16 Silver St. Also at, 23 Wellinborough Rd, Finedon, Wellingborough, Northants.
Kb; Special Smokeless Cartridge.

ARTHUR JAMES RUDD. [Gm]. Ad; 54 London St, Norwich.
Also at, 17 Regent St, Great Yarmouth, Norfolk.
Kb; The Norfolk, Rudd's Standard, Rudd's Star Cartridge (shown Above), Rudd's X.L. Cartridge.

ALEXANDER JOHN RUSSELL. Later as, A. J. RUSSELL & SONS. [Gm].
Ad; 32 High St, Maidstone, Kent.
Kb; The Reliance Smokeless, Russell's Special.

JAMES RUSSELL. [Im]. Ad; Elgin, Moray (Grampian).
Kb; Un.

ALFRED H. RUTT. [Gm]. Ad; Cattle Market. Also at,
9 George Row, Northampton, Northants.
Kb; Un (shown above).

H. F. SALE & SON.   Ad; Shipston-on-Stour, Warw.
Kb; Champion, Rover, The Saleson (shown above).

W. SAMPLE. [Gd and ammunition]. Ad; Amble, Northumberland.
Kb; Un.

ALFRED SANDERS. [Gm]. Ad; 79 Bank St, Maidstone, Kent.
Kb; The Allington, Eley's gas-tight Cartridge Case, Fourten,
Invicta Special, Long Tom, The Medway, Un (shown above).
Rm; Established in 1838. At a later date they took over the
Business of Swinfen. They also sold pinfire cartridges.

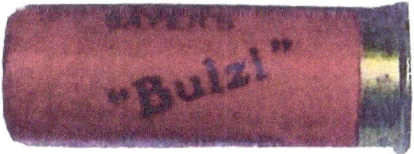 

SAYER.   [Gm]. Ad; Watton, Norfolk.
Kb; Sayer's Bulzi.

 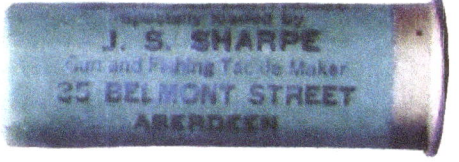 

J. S. SHARPE. [Gun and fishing tackle dealer]. Ad; 35 Belmont St,
Aberdeen, Aberdeens (Grampian).
Kb; The Buchan, The Scottie.

SCHULTZE CO. Also known as, SCHULTZE GUNPOWDER CO LTD. [Am, Pm]. Ad; 3 Bucklersbury. Also at, 28 & 32 Gresham St. And also, 40 New Broad St, London EC.
Kb; The Albion, The Bomo, The Captain (Captain E. Schultze), The Caro, The Conqueror, Cube Powder Cartridge, Deep Brass Gastight, Ejector, The Eyeworth, Grand Prix, Nitro, The Pickaxe, Rainproof, The Rufus Smokeless Cartridge, Schultze Smokeless Powder, The Toro, Waterproof, The Westminster, The Yeoman.
Rm; The Schultze Co was formed in Great Britain in 1868 with their powder mill at Eyeworth Lodge, New Forest, Hants. In 1909 a separate company was formed. See Cogschultze Ammunition & Powder Co Ltd, in this book. Schultze finally merged with Messrs Eley Bros circa 1911. Several of the firms cartridges took their names from their powders.

SHAW & CO. [Gm and stores]. Ad; West Meath, Mullingar, Republic of Ireland.
Kb; Nobel's Sporting Ballistite (Shaw's name on the tube).

EDWARD LEADER SHEPHERD. [Gm, Im]. Ad; High St. Also in, Lombard St, Abingdon, Berks (Oxon).
Kb; Eley's Ejector (Shepherd's name on top card only).

SKINNER & CO.   Ad; 62 Derby St. Also At, 63 Haywood St, Leek, Staffs.
Kb; Champion Smokeless Cartridge, Un (shown above).

SLINGSBY BROTHERS. Later as, SLINGSBY GUNS. [Gm].
Ad; 10 High St, Boston. Also at, Sleaford, Lincs.
Kb; Slingsby's Champion, Slingsby's Fen, Slingsby's Special, Slingsby's Stump Cartridge (shown above).

JOHN SMAIL & SONS. [Im]. Ad; Morpeth, Northumberland.
Kb; The Lightning Killer.

PETER SMALL. [Gm or Gs]. Ad; 38 Pilgrim St, Newcastle-upon-Tyne, Northumberland (Tyne & Wear).
Kb; Burnand Cartridge, Kynoch's Grouse Ejector.

ALFRED FISHER SMITH. Ad; High St, Hailsham. Also at, High St, Heathfield, Suseex
Kb; The Hailsham Special, Yellow Boy (drawing shown above).

CHARLES SMITH. Later as, CHAS SMITH & SONS. [Gm].
Ad; 37 Market St. Later at, 47 Market Place, Also at, 28 Milton St, Newark, Notts.
Kb; All British Extra Special, The Castle, The Clinton, Extra Special Cartridge, Kynoch's Grouse Ejector, The Newark, The Rufford, Schultze Load, Universal, Un.

EDWARD H. SMITH & SONS. [Im]. Ad; 2 Market Place, Brigg, Lincs.
Kb; The Lightning (shown above).

STEVE SMITH. [Gs]. Ad; 42 High Friar St, Newcastle-under-Lyme, Staffs.
Kb; Trap and Game (shown above).
Rm; Produced by Greenwood & Batley. Later were closed by crimping.

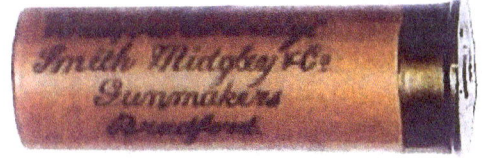 

SMITH MIDGLEY. Later as, SMITH MIDGLEY & CO. [Gm].
Ad; 25 Sunbridge Rd, Bradford, Yorks.
Kb; The Bradford Cartridge, Pegamoid, Un.

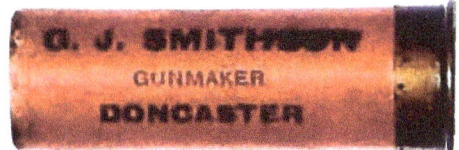

G. J. SMITHSON.   Ad; Doncaster, Yorks.
Kb; Un.

 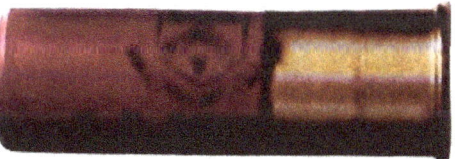 

J. F. SMYTHE LTD. [Gm, Cl]. Ad; The Sportsman's Repository, Darlington.
Also at, Dovecot St, Stockton-on-Tees, County Durham (Cleveland).
Kb; Durham Ranger, Eley's Ejector, The Field Cartridge, Gastight, Smythe's
Champion, Smythe's Express, Smythe's Special Load.

H. & R. SNEEZUM. [Gm]. Ad; 14, 16, 18, 20 Fore St, Ipswich, Suffolk.
Kb; Sneezum's Anglia (shown above), Sneezum's Special High Velocity Load.

SOUTHERN REMEDIAL SERVICES. [Treatments in risen damp and woodworm]. Kb; Un.

JOHN WILLIAM & EDWIN SOWMAN LTD. [Im, general furnishing, cycle agents and seed merchants]. Ad; Olney, Bucks.
Kb; The Hare, The Keeper, The Pheasant, The Sureshot Smokeless (shown above).

ALFRED L. SPENCER. [Gm]. Ad; Finkle St, Richmond, Yorks.
Kb; Un.
Rm; Also in Richmond there was a Charles Spencer at 5 Finkle St and I also have an Ad for him at Field St. An over shot card has also been seen that was printed, A. A. Spencer.Richmond.

STANBURY & STEVENS. [Gun and cartridge experts].
Ad; 14 Alphington St, St Thomas, Exeter, Devon.
Kb; The Devonia, The Game, The Ideal, The Monocle, The Red Flash (shown above), The Standby, The Swift.

STEBBINGS & SON. [Gun and ammubition dealers].
Ad; Attleborough, Norfolk.
Kb; Specal Smokeless (pheasant on tube, shown above).

THOMAS STENSBY. Later as, T. STENSBY & CO. [Gm and rifle maker, Cl].
Ad; 20 Hanging Ditch. Later, 6 Withy Grove. And later, 12 Withy Grove, Manchester (Gt Manchester).
Kb; The All British, The Champion Cartridge, The Champion Gastight, The Club All British, Pegamoid, The Victory, Un.   Rm; Established 1810.

STERLING.   Ad; London (Rest of address not known).
Kb; Sterling Black Powder, Sterling Ejector, Sterling Extra Primer, Sterling Smokeless. Un.

STILES BROS. [Im]. Ad; 39 High St. Later at, 51 Market Place, Warminster, Wilts.
Kb; The Kill Quick (shown above).
Rm; These brothers were known active in Warminster in 1907. The firm closed their Market Place shop in April 1987.

JOHN STREET & SONS. [Im]. Ad; Castle St, Christchurch. Also at, 95 Christchurch Rd, Boscombe, Hants.
Kb; Un (name on over shot card).

J. STRONG & SON. [Gun and ammunition dealers]. Ad; 65 Castle St. Also at, 8 Warwick Rd, Carlisle, Cumberland (Cumbria).
Kb; Un.

J. SWINFEN. [Gm]. Ad; 79 Bank St, Maidstone, Kent.
Kb; Eley's Gas-tight Cartridge Case (Swinfen's name on the stamping, shown above), Swinfen's Special.

 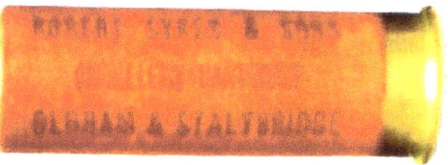 

ROBERT SYKES & SONS LTD.   Ad; Oldham. Also in, Stalybridge,
Lancs, (Great Manchester).
Kb; Smokeless Cartridge.

SYKES BROS. Ad; Queen St, Ossett, Yorks.
Kb; Ballistite Cartridge, Eley Ejector (Syke's name on over shot card, Shown above).

 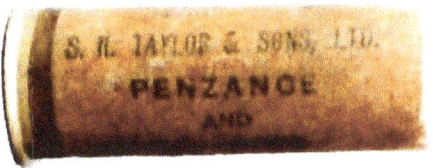

S.R. TAYLOR & SONS. Ad; Penzance. Also at St Ives, Cornwall.
Kb; Un.

TAYLOR & JONES. Ad; Monmouth, Mon (Gwent).
Also at, Ross-on-Wye, Herefs (Hereford & Worcester).
Kb; The Monno Cartridge (shown above).

 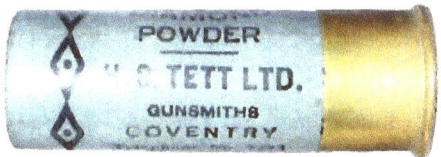 

H. G. TETT. [Gs]. Ad; Coventry, Warw (West Midlands).
Kb; Un.

R. THRIPLAND & SON.   Ad; Galashields, Selkirkshire (Borders).
Kb; Eley Grand Prix Case, Special Smokeless, Un (shown above).
Rm; Thripland's name seen on the over shot cards.

WILLIAM HENRY CLAYTON THURMAN. [Im]. Ad; 17 South St, Dorchester, Dorset
Kb; Nk.
Rm; The above provisional drawing was made from metal detected remains. He was known active at the above Ad in 1889. By 1907 the Ad was, Thurman W.H.C. (W.R. Skyrme Successor). By 1927 the Ad was, Thurman (J.E. Skyrme Proprietor).

ROBERT TILNEY & SON. [Gm]. Ad; 17 Smallgate St, Beccles, Suffolk.
Kb; The Beccles Cartridge, Eley Pegamoid Patent (name only on shot Card, Tilney's Special Smokeless.

JOHN TISDALL. {Gm]. Ad; 8 South St, Chichester. Also at, High St, Arundel, Sussex.
Kb; The Chichester Cartridge.

TRENT GUN & CARTRIDGE WORKS. [Am, Cl, Wm]. Ad; Wellholme Rd. Also At, Fairfield, Grimsby, Lincs (Humberside).
Kb; A.E.C. Rook, Best Smokeless, Deep Shell, Favourite, London, Smokeless Air Lord, Spartan, Spartan Deep Shell, Super Range, Un.
Rm; Also loaded for other firms. Spartan range for Cartridge Syndicate Ltd.

 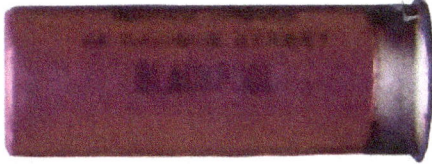 

STEPHEN TROUGHTON. [Gm]. Ad; 24 Caunce St, Blackpool, Lancs.
Kb; Un (pheasant on tube).

Squared turn-over

TRULOCK BROTHERS. [Gm]. Ad; 13 Parliament St, Dublin, Republic of Ireland.
Kb;Eley's Gas-tight Cartridge, Reliable Smokeless (drawing shown above).

TRULOCK & HARRISS. Later in Dublin as, TRULOCK, HARRISS & RICHARDSON LTD. [Gm]. Ad; 9 Dawson St, Dublin, Republic of Ireland. As TRULOCK & HARRISS also at, Pickering Place, St James's St, London W1.   Kb; E.C. Powder Cartridge, Kynoch Grouse Ejector, Nobel's Empire (crossed flags), Nobel's Sporting Ballistite, The Tru-iss, Un.

J. TUCKER. [Gs and sports outfitter]. Ad; 25 Bailey St, Oswestry, Salop.
Kb; The Oswestrian (shown above).

 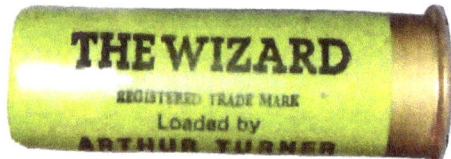 

ARTHUR TURNER. Later as, ARTHUR TURNER (SHEFFIELD) LTD. [Gm].
Kb; The Alliance, The Clay Bird, The Double Wing, The Steeltown, The Wing, The Wizard (shown above),   Rm; Arthur took over the business from Maleham & Co in the 1920's and retained some of their brand names.

 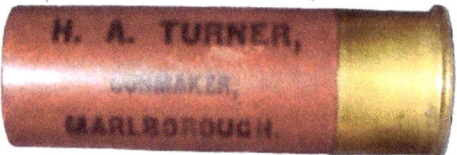 

HENRY A. TURNER. Later as, H. A. TURNER LTD. [Gm].
Ad; 142 High St. Also at, Bath Rd, Marlborough, Wilts.
Kb; The Kennett, Un (one of several shown above).
Rm; Both his Ad were active in the late 1890's.

THOMAS TURNER & SON. Later, T. TURNER & SONS LTD. [Gm, Lm].
Ad; 8 Butter Market, Reading; 86 Northbrook St, Newbury, Berks; 35 Wote St, Basingstoke, Hants: Kb; Un, British Wonders, Craven, Fillbag, Grey Rapid, Grouse Ejector, Midget, Penwood, Renowned, Special Loading, Smokeless Wonder.

 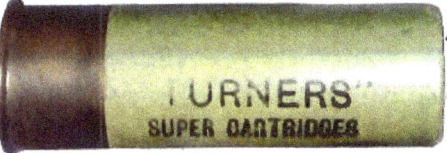 

TURNER'S CARBIDES LTD. [Dealers and merchants in cabide lighting].
Ad; 58 De Grey St, Hull, Yorks (Humberside).
Kb; The 410, The Killer, The Standard, The Super, Turner's Super Cartridges (shown above).   Rm; Formed in 1924 by the father of two Sons that were directors of the Hull Cartridge Co Ltd.

F. TURVEY. Later as, F. TURVEY & SONS. [Sports, gun and ammunition dealers]. Ad; 2 Woodhall St. Also at, Sert St, Bury St Edmunds, Suffolk.
Kb; Turvey's Deadcert.

JOHN TYLER. Later as, J. TYLER (HIGHBRIDGE) LTD. [Gun and Ammunition dealer]. Ad; Highbridge, Somerset.
Kb; The Falcon (shown above), The Special.

 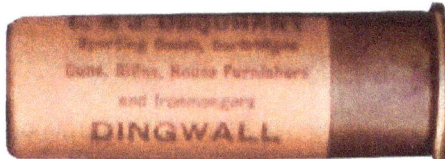 

C. & J. URQUHART. [Im, gun dealers]. Ad; Dingwall, Ross & Cromarty (Highland).
Kb; The Ardross Cartridge (shown above).

W. URTON
CHESTERFIELD

WILLIAM URTON LTD. [Im, may have been Gs]. Ad; Glunmangate. Later at, 7 West Bars and Park Rd, Chesterfield, Derbys.
Kb; Un (perhaps known as, The Spire. Shown above).
Rm; Listed in 1881 as being at Glunmangate. A1932 directory listed them at other Ad's.

JOHN VENABLES & SON. [Gm and rifle]. Ad; 99 St Aldate's St, Oxford, Oxen.
Kb; 410 Long, 410 Short, The County, The Gastight, The Oxford, The Sixteen, Special Smokeless Metal Lined, Un (including centre and pinfire).

R. H. WAGSTAFF & CO. [Im and ammunition dealers].
Ad; 16 New St. Also at, 22 Winchester St, Basingstoke, Hants.
Kb; A.1. (shown above).
Rm; Known to have been active in 1898. Their main premises were destroyed In the great fire of Basingstoke on 17th April 1905.

DERRIAN WALES. [Gm, Im]. Ad; 16 Regent St, Great Yarmouth, Norfolk.
Kb; Un (shown above).

F. E. WALKER. [Gm]. Ad; 11 Cheap St, Newbury, Berks.
Kb; No known cartridge..
Rm; There was a Gm named G.E. Walker at 86 Northbrook St, Newbury prior to Thos Turner & Sons at that address. There may have been family connections. The above provisional drawing has been made from metal detected remains.

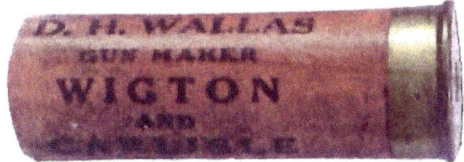 

D. H. WALLAS. [Gm, Cl]. Ad; Carlisle. Also at, Wigton, Cumberland (Cumbria).
Kb; Un.

WALLIS BROS. [Gm, Locksmiths, Cycle agents, Electrical engineers, Contactors, Bell hangers]. Ad; 156 High St. Also at, 364 High St. Also at, 1 Cornhill. Later at, 4 St Mary's St, Lincoln, Lincs.
Kb; The Big Tom of Lincoln (named after a bell in the cathedral), Gastight Cartridge Case, Smokeless Cartridge, Walbro Special.

WANLESS BROS. [Gm]. Ad; Russell St. Later at, 66 Ocean Rd, South Shields. Also at, 20 Norfolk St, Also at, Waterloo Place, Sunderland. And also at, 95 High St, Stockton-on-Tees, County Durham (Tyne & Wear).
Kb; Kynoch's Perfectly Gas-tight, The Long Range, Pegamoid, The Waterloo, The W.B.S., The Weardale..

WANLESS & CO. [Gm and rifle]. Ad; South Shields, County Durham (Tyne & Wear).
Kb; The Long Range (shown above), The Perfect.

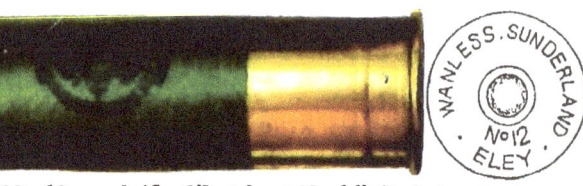

WILLIAM WANLESS. [Gm and rifle, Cl]. Ad; 29 Norfolk St. Later at, 20 Norfolk St. Also at 22 St Thomas St, Sunderland, County Durham (Tyne & Wear).
Kb; Kynoch's Perfectly Gas-tight, The Long Range.
Rm; The Wanless firms mention must have had a family connection. I do not Know of their histories and so I have entered them separately.

J.WARD & SON. [Domestic engineers, Im and furnishings].
Ad; 21 Broad St. Also at, 89 High St, Worcester, Worcs (H & W).
Kb; Kynoch Patent Grouse Ejector (shown above).

A. WARD THOMPSON. Later as, WARD THOMPSON BROS. [Gm].
Ad; 99 Corporation Rd. Later at, 87 Borough Rd, Middlesborough, Yorks (Cleveland). Also at, Stockton-on-Tees, County Durham (Cleveland).
Kb; Un.

 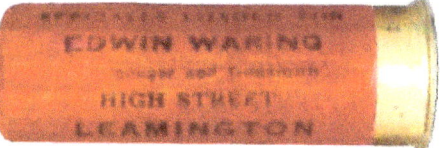 

EDWIN WARING. [Gs, Im]. Ad; High St, Leamington Spa, Warw.
Kb; Un (shown above).

 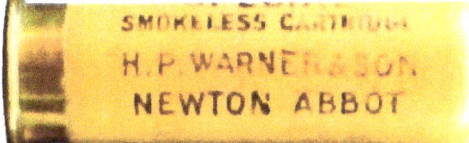 

HENRY P. WARNER & SON. [Im]. Ad; 11 Bank St, Newton Abbot, Derby.
Kb; General Service Cartridge (Mullerite with extra tube printing,
High Velocity Special Smokeless (shown above).

JOHN WARRICK. [Manufacturer of cycles and motor tradesmans
Tricycles]. Ad; 34 St Mary's Butts. Also at, Monarch Works,
Caversham Rd, Reading, Berks.
Kb; Un.

JAMES BAKEWELL WARRILOW. [Gs, Cl]. Ad; Factory Lane,
Chippenham, Wilts.
Kb; Badminton, Ejector, Electric Long Shot (shown above), The Good Sport,
Sudden Death.
Rm; Was known to have been active in Chippenham circa, 1886-1913.

THOMAS J. WATKINS. Later as, WATKINS & CO. [Gm].
Ad; High St, Banbury, Oxon.
Kb; Special Loading (drawing shown above). Un.

WATSON BROTHERS. [Gm]. Ad; 29 Old Bond St.
Also at, Pall Mall, London SW1.
Kb; Hi-Speed Cartridge, Non-recoil Smokeless,
Reliance (shown above). Rm; Were known active
in 1901. Later were absorbed into Grant & Lang.

JAS R. WATSON & CO. Ad; 35 Queen Victoria St, London EC4. [Ga, Cl].
Kb; The Albion, The Britannia, The Challenge, Ejector, The Enterprise, Gastight
Cone Base, The Lilliput, The Sureshot, The Warrior, The Wettern.
Rm; Established 1889. Most of their brands were in Belgium cases loaded with
Cooppal powders. These were-, Black Powders; Treble Strong and F. Smokeless
Sportings; No 1 and Emerald (granular). No 2 and Excelsior (leaflet). Customers
Ordering 10,000 and upwards could if wished have their names printed on them.

 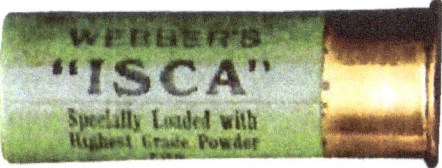 

J. WEBBER & SONS. [[Sports depot]]. Ad; Exeter, Torquay & Newton Abbot, Devon.
Kb; Webber's ISCA.

WEBBERS.   Ad; New St, Honiton, Devon.
Kb; The Ottervale Special Smokeless (shown above).

  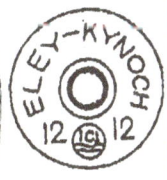

G. R. WEBSTER.   Ad; 30A Wide Bargate, Boston, Lincs.
Kb; The Favourite, The Field (shown above), The Snipe.

 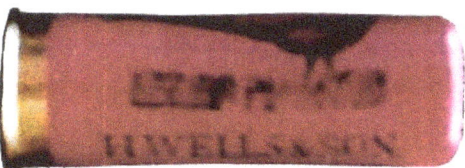 

H. WELLS & SON. [Gun, ammunition dealer]. Ad; Ware, Herts.
Kb; Un.

WILLIAM WELSH.   Ad; Dumfries, Dumfries-shire (Dumfries & Galloway).
Also at, Castle Douglas, Kirkudbright (Dumfies & Galloway.
Kb; Queen of the South (drawing shown above).

MRS ELIZA WEST. Later as, WEST & SON. [Gm]. 3 Grove St, East
Retford. Later at, 26 Market Square & 10 Bridge Gate St, Retford, Notts.
Kb; The County, Deep Shell, Ejector, Four-10, The Grand National
(shown above), The Sherwood, Waterproof Pegamoid, Un.
Rm; Traded as E. West circa 1881-1894. As West & Son from 1912 onwards.

WEST LONDON SHOOTING SCHOOL. [Shooting tuition].
Ad; Perivale, Ealing, London W.
Kb; Empire (shown above), Un.

WEST & SON. [Gs]. Ad; Great Yarmouth, Norfolk.
Kb; Norfolk High Velocity Load (shown above).

 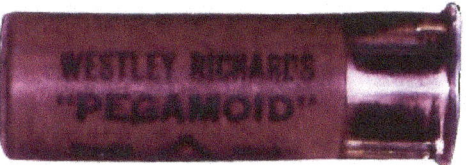 

 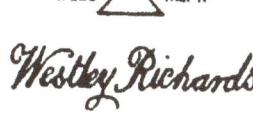

WESTLEY RICHARDS & CO LTD. [Gm, Cl]. Ad; 12 Corporation St. Later at, 24 Bennett's Hill, Birmingham, Warw (W. Midlands). Also at, New Bond St. And later, 23 Conduit St, London W1.
Kb; The A.L.P. Cartridge, The Aquatite, The Carlton, The Explora (hollow slug cartridge), The Fauneta (ball loaded), Pegamoid, The Regent (ejector metal covered), The Right & Left, The Special, Super Magnum Explora, Special Accelerated L.P. Loading, The Wizard.
Rm; November 1910, made a move from Corporation St, to Bennett's Hill. September 1917, made a move from , New Bond St, to Conduit St. Their Wizard was sold at their West Hendon Shooting School.

CHARLES & HERBERT WESTON. [Later became, C. & A. WESTON. [Gm]. Ad; The Colonade. Also at, 7 New Rd, Brighton. Was also at, Hailsham, Sussex.
Kb; Brighton, Colonade, Ejector, National Smokeless, Smokeless Cartridge, Special Smokeless, Un.   Rm, Their business terminated in the 1970's.

T. WHALEY & SON. [Im, agricultural equipment dealers].
Ad; Bridge St, St Ives, Cambridgeshire.
Kb; Eley Bros's Grand Prix (Whaley's name on over shot card only), Mullerite Smokeless (extra tube printings, drawing shown above), Un.
Rm; They also sold Kynoch brands.

JOHN EDWARD WHITEHOUSE. Later as, J. E. WHITEHAOUSE & SONS. [Gm]. Ad; High St, Oakham, Rutland (Leics).
Kb; The Quorn, The Rutland (shown above).

WHITEMAN BROS LTD. [Cl]. Ad; Silver St, Worcester, Worcs (H & W).
Kb; The Rapid (shown above).

FRANK SIDNEY WHITEMAN. [Gs, Im]. Ad; 20-21 Market Place, Wallingford, Berks (Oxon).
Kb; The Fordian (F. Dyke load).
Rm; Known to have been active between 1928 and 1939 and possibly for longer.

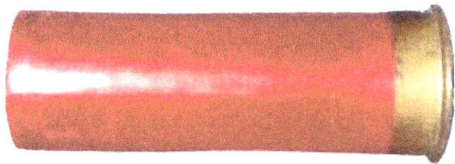

H. H. WHITNEY.   Ad; Newtown ? (Rest of Ad not known).
Kb; Un (name on over shot card only. Shown above).

H. W. WILDMAN. [Gun and sports]. Ad; High St, Ledbury, Herts (H & W).
Kb; Un.

JOHN WILKES. {Gun and sports]. Ad; 1 Lower St, St James's,
Piccadilly Circus. Later to, 79 Beak St, London W1.
Kb; Tom-Tom (shown above).
Rm; First in business in Birmingham. Moved to London in 1879 and
joined forces with Dalziel Dougal & Son at 59 St James's St.

WILKINSONS. [Sports store]. Ad; Penrith, Cumberland (Cumbria).
Kb; The Beacon, The Eden.

WILLIAMS & POWELL. [Gm, rifle and pistol]. Ad; 27 South Castle St,
Liverpool, Lancs (Merseyside). Also in London, the Ad not known.
Kb; The Castle, Kynoch's Grouse Ejector (Willam & Powell's name
on the stampings.

CLARRIE WILSON. [Pc]. Ad; Kinder, The Peak, Derbys.
Kb; Clarrie Wilson (shown above).

F. K. WILSON & CO. [Im]. Ad; Stokesley, Yorks.
   Kb; Eley Bros EBL Shield Cartridge (pluss Wilson's name), Un.

J. WILSON & SONS. [Im]. Ad; 169-171 South St, St Andrews, Fife.
Kb; High Velocity (shown above).

JAMES WILSON. Later as, JAMES WILSON & SONS. [Gn].
Ad; 47 Goodramgate, York, Yorks.
Kb; Eley's Ejector, Own Loading.

WILLIAMSON. Later as, WILLIAMSON & SON. [Gm or Gs].
Ad; 34 The Bull Ring, Ludlow, Salop.
Kb; Un (Williamson's name on top card only).

 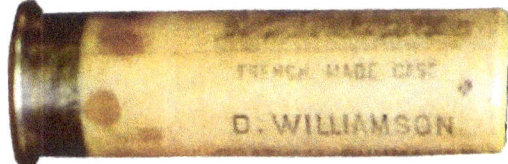

D. WILLIAMSON. [Gm]. Ad; 3-5 Waterloo Bridge Rd, London WC2.
Kb; Ejector, Un.

RICHARD WISE. [Im]. Ad; 10 The Bull Ring, Kidderminster,
Worcs (H&W Hereford & Worcester).
Kb; The Lightning Cartridge.

ARTHUR WOOD (NEWPORT I.W.). [Gs, Im]. Ad; 114 Pyle St, Newport,
Isle of Wight.
Kb; Demon, Un,
Rm; Arthur ceased trading in the 1960's.

R. J. WOODROW. [Im]. Ad; High St, Brandon, Suffolk.
Kb; The Champion Smokeless Cartridge (shown above).

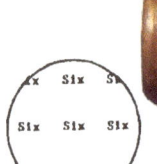  

EDMUND WOODS. [Gm]. Ad; 36 Bow St, London.
Kb; Un (Wood's name on the stamping. Shown above).
Rm; Edmund was active between 1864 and 1891.

GEORGE L. WOODS. Later as, G. L. WOODS & SONS. [Gm, Cl].
Ad; Ovington, Norfolk.
Kb; Castle Forbes, Norfolk Universal, Woods Special, Woods Supreme, Un.
Rm; Loaded for private orders like country estates. Some other brands are not shown here as they were crimped closed.

JAMES WOODWARD & SONS. [Gm]. Ad; 64 St James's St, Pall Mall.
Also at, 29 Bury St, St James's, London W1.
Kb; The Automatic, Eley Ejector, Kynoch Patent Grouse Ejector,
Patent Gastight, Special Smokeless, Un.

RALPH WOOLISCROFT. [Im]. Ad; 12 Derby St, Leek, Staffs.
Kb; Eley's E.B. Nitro Cartridge Case (Wooliscroft's name on brass Stamping. Shown above).

GEORGE WREN. [Im and saddler]. Ad; High St, Hungerford, Berks.
Also in, Ramsbury, Wilts.
Kb; Hungerford (drawing shown above, Un pinfire (Wren's name was only on the over shot card).   Rm; Directoties show this firm as Wren & Matthews circa 1869-1877. George sold out in 1925.

RANDALL WRIGHT. [Gs]. Ad; Spalding, Lincs,
Kb; Amberite Cartridge.

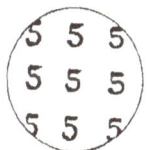  

A. B. WYLIE. [Cl, Im]. Ad; 64-66 Market Place. Also at Theatre St, Warwick, Warw.
Kb; The Killklean.
Rm; I was once shown their old loading machine. Alas, not a cartridge Or case was left in the place.

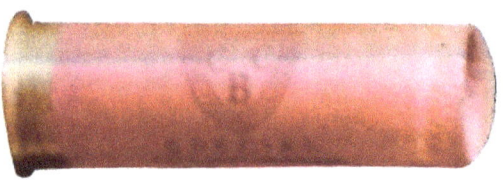

C. C. B.   Firm and their Ad not known.
Kb; Crown Brand.
Rm; Note the look-a-like to the shield and the stamping to that of Eley.

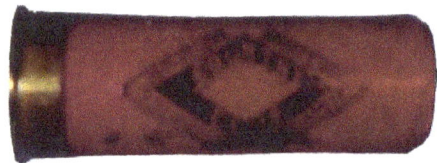

THE COUNTRY CLUB. Ad; Not known. (I have no other information).
Kb; Country Club Made in England (shown above).

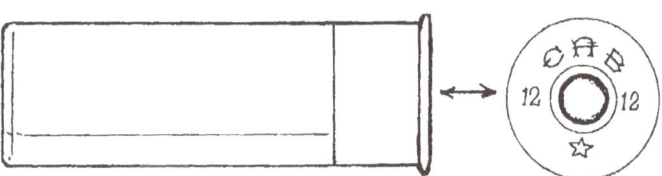

C R B. No other details are known.
The above headstamping shown was drawn from cartridge remains that were
Found by metal detecting.

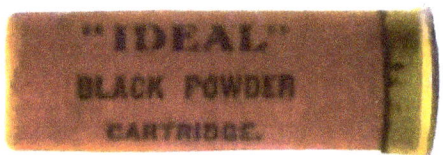

IDEAL.   Ad; London. (I have no other information).
Kb; Ideal Black Powder Cartridge (shown above).

A few of the unidentified.

LODA. Firm and their Ad not known.
Kb; Loda.

SPEEDWAY. Ad; Not known
Kb; Speedway Cartridge.

THE TROJAN. Ad; Not known.
Kb; The Trojan (shown above).

THE UNION JACK BRAND. Ad; Not known. (I have no other information).
Kb; The Union Jack Brand (shown above).
Rm; The motifs shown are each on a different cartridge.

A few of the unidentified.

SECTION THREE
Additional drawings to those in the book
STAMPINGS on SHOTSHELLS

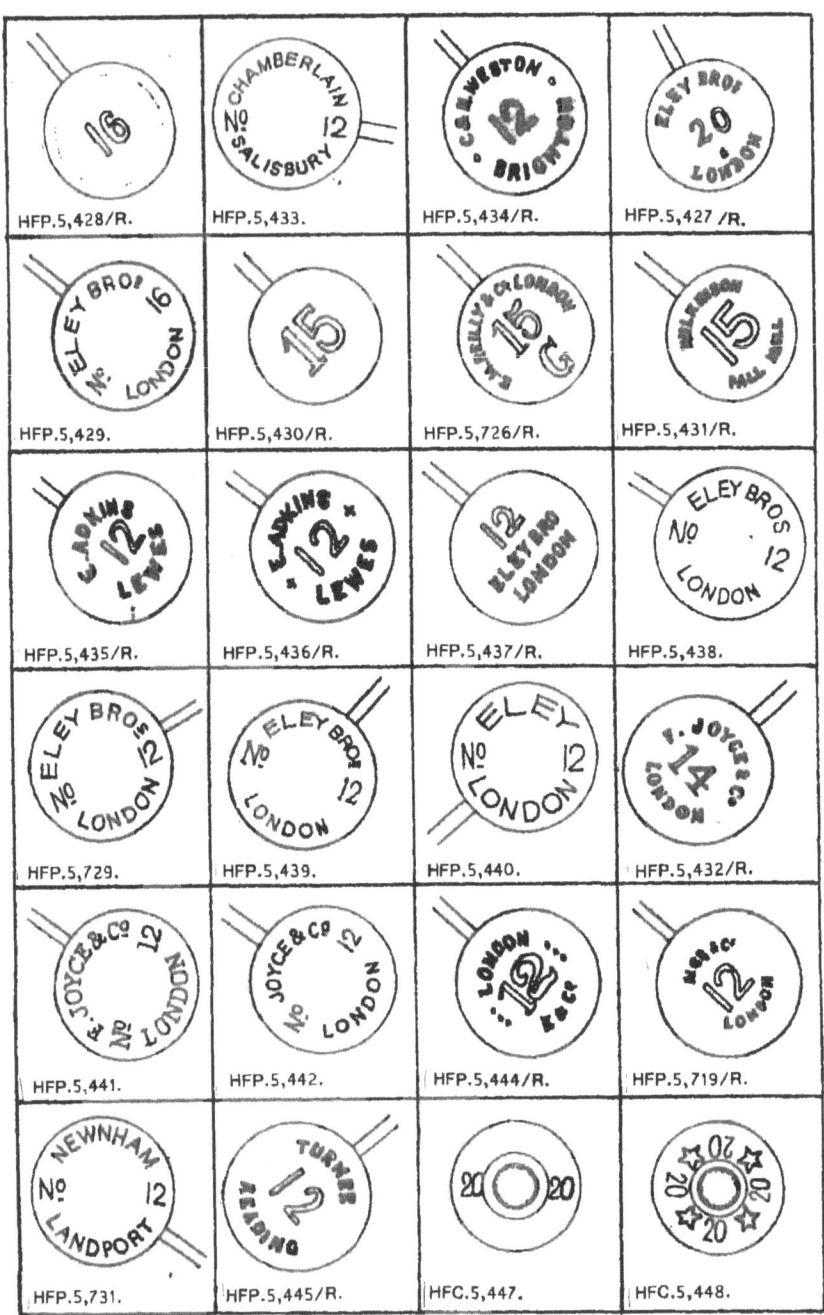

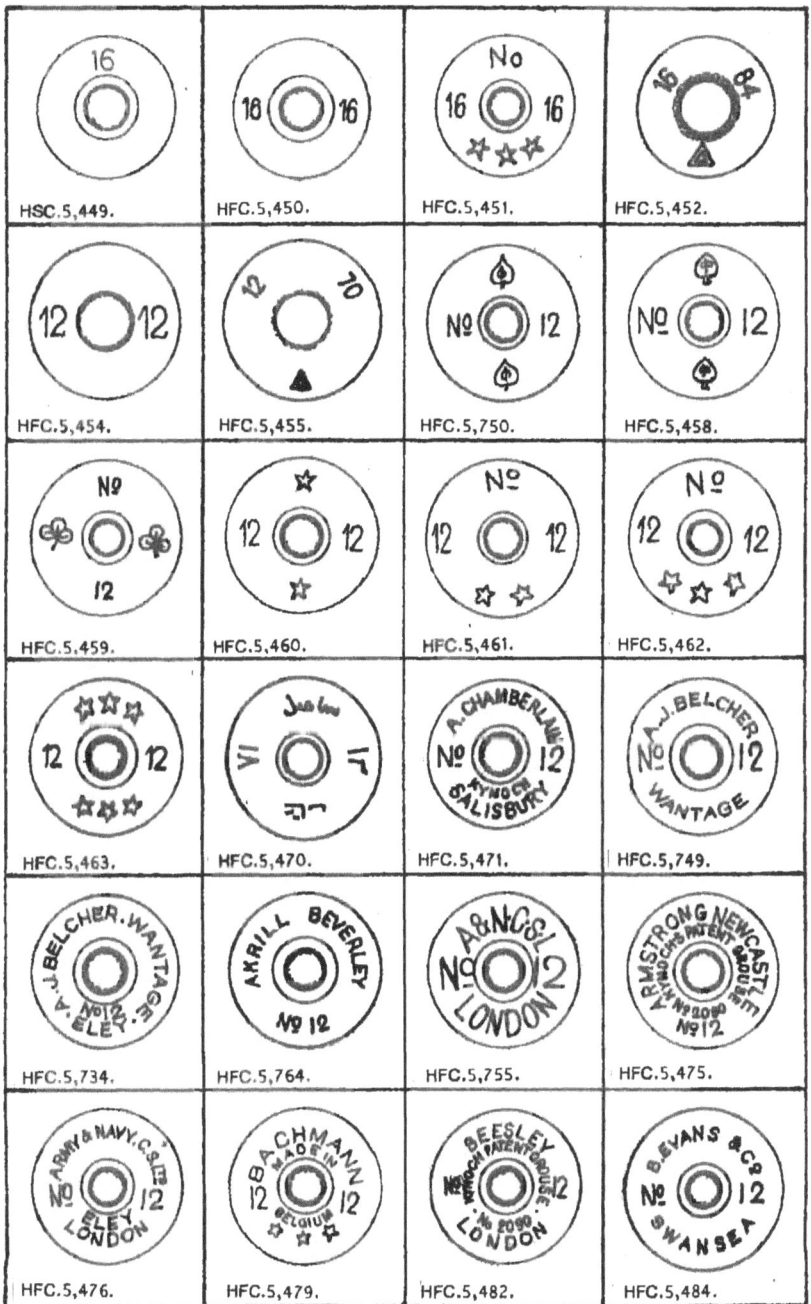

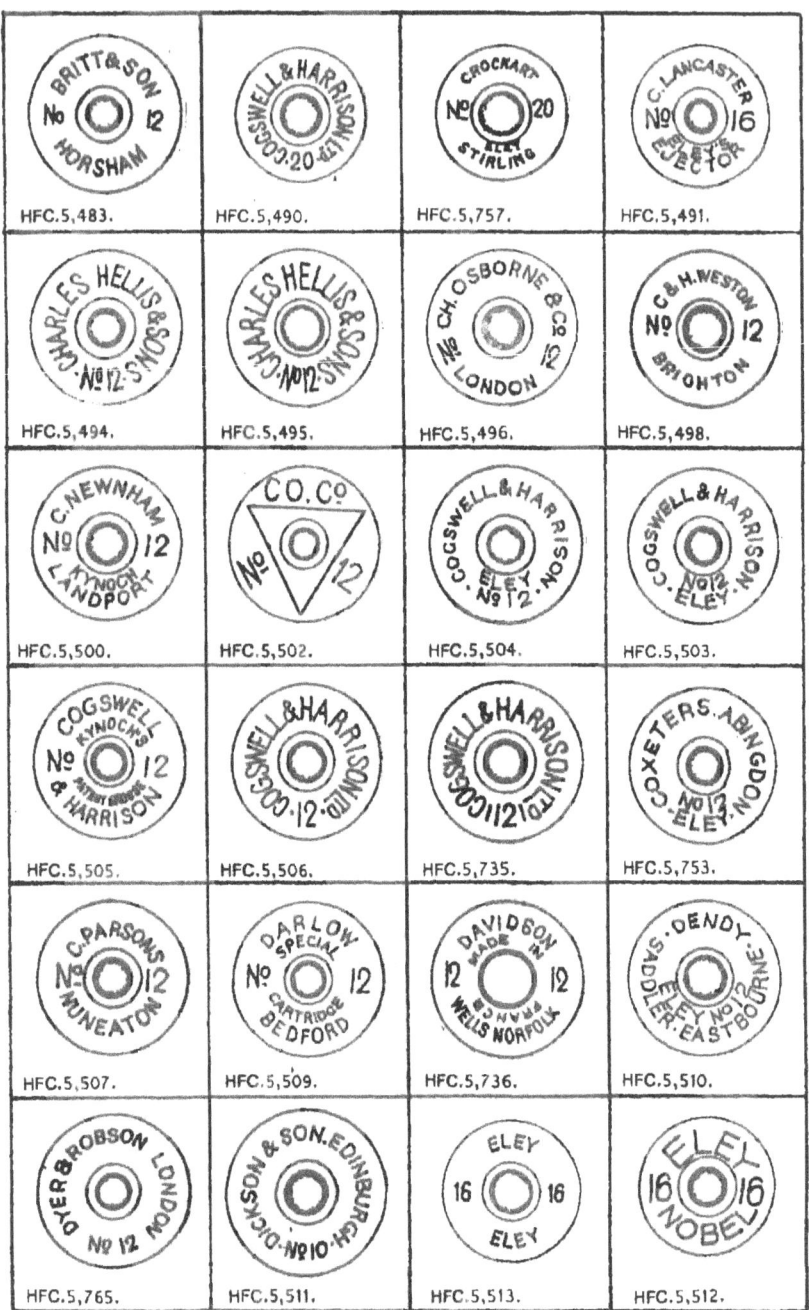

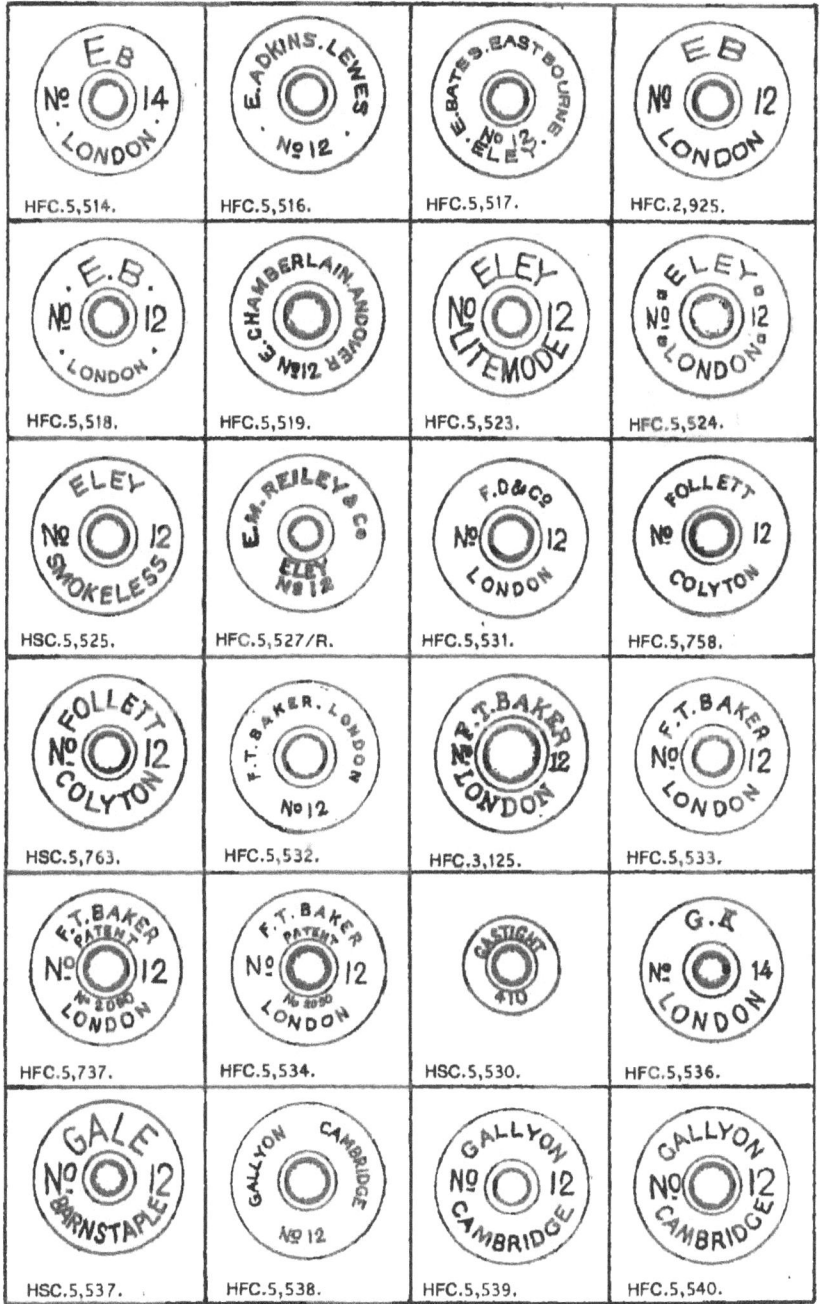

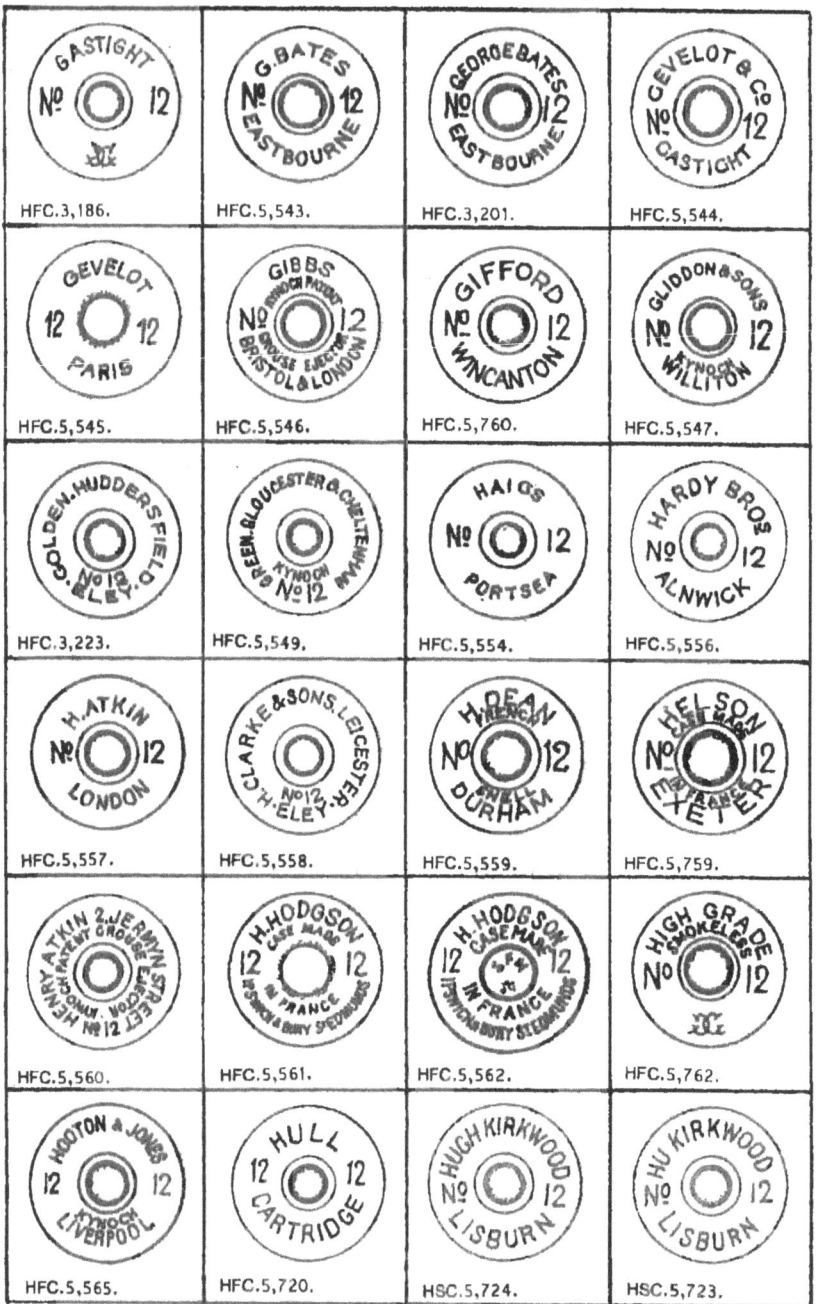

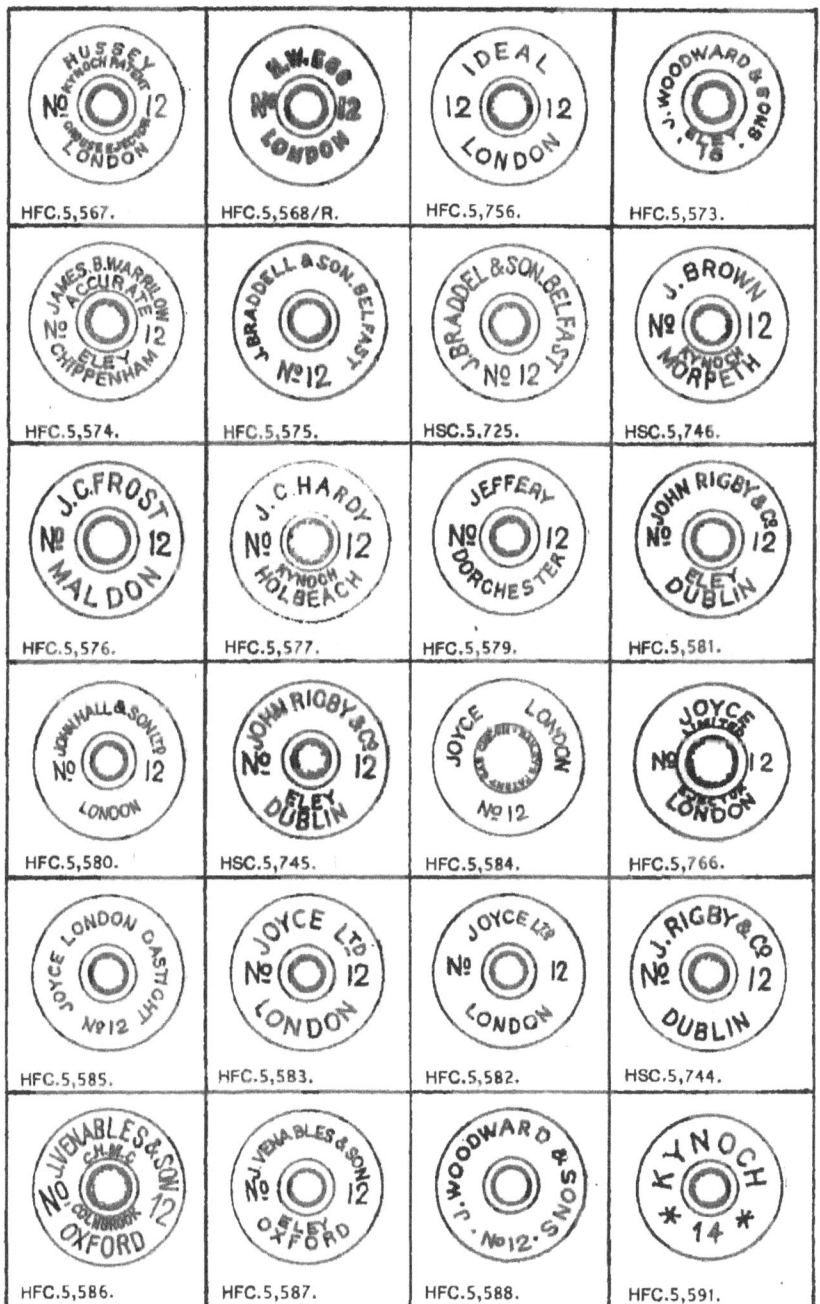

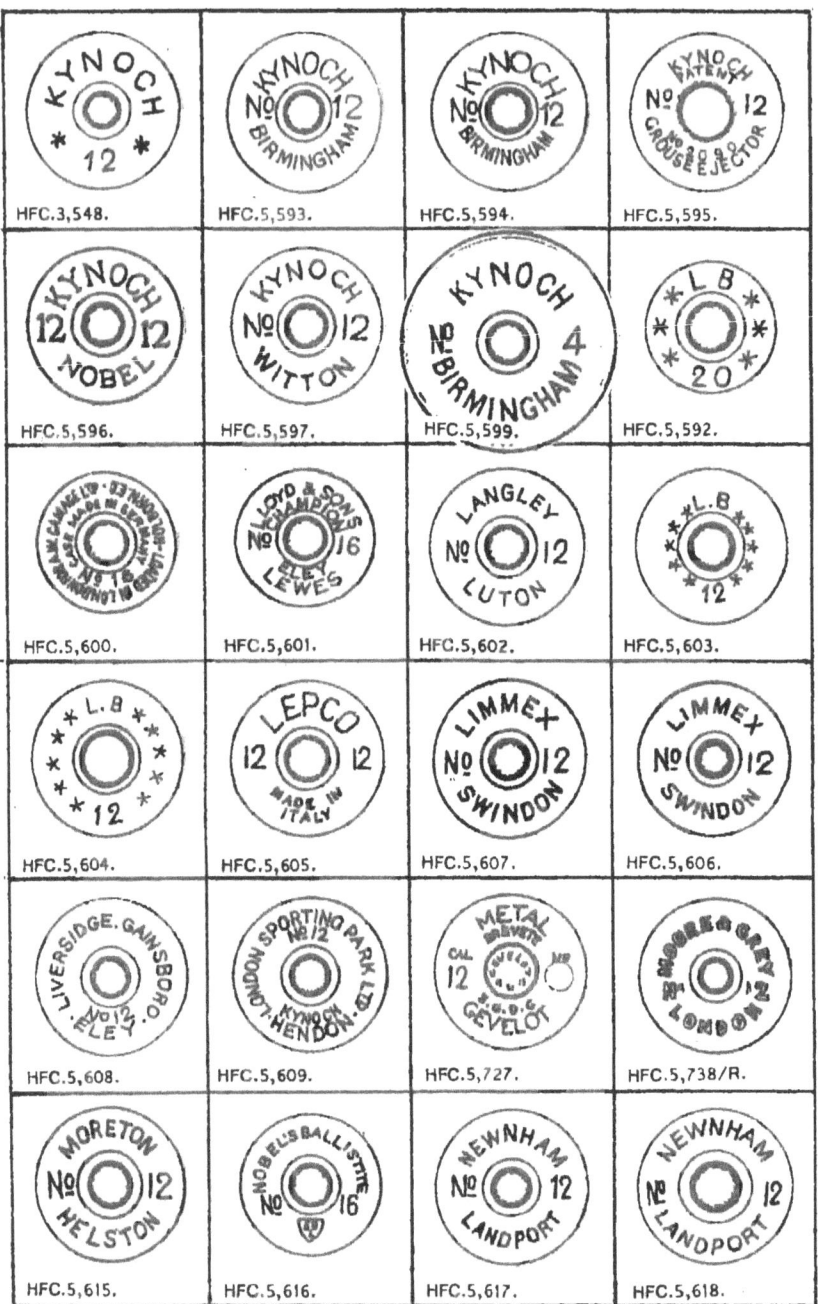

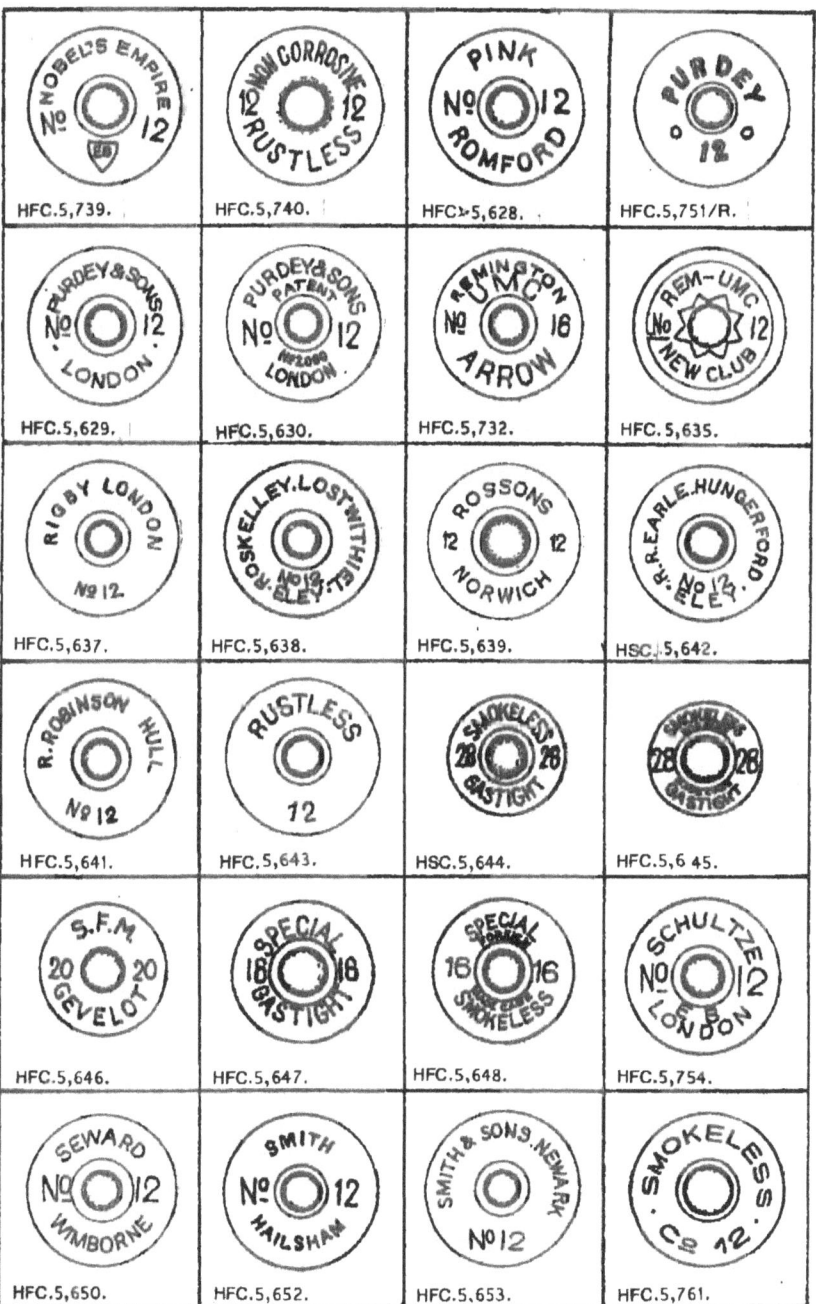

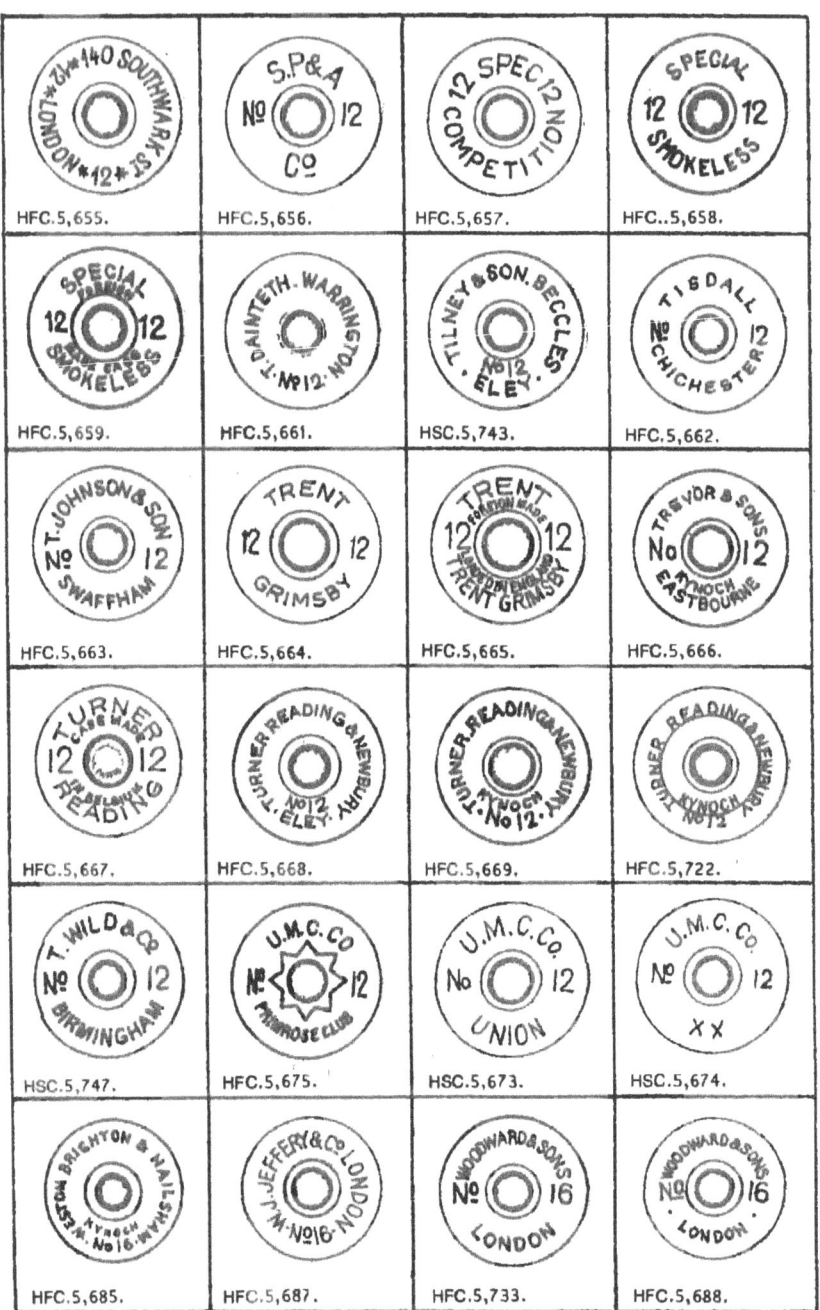

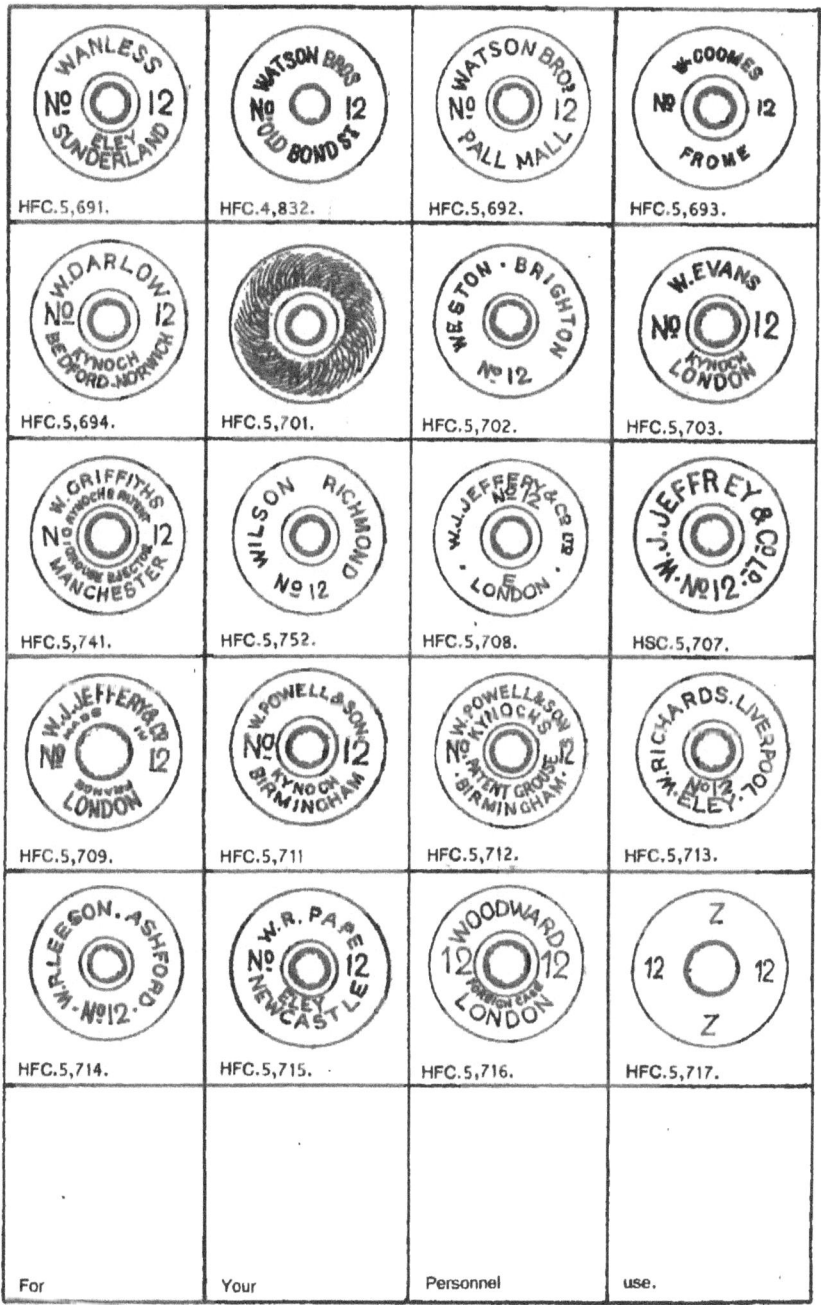

www.ingramcontent.com/pod-product-compliance
Lightning Source LLC
Chambersburg PA
CBHW040250170426
43191CB00018B/2362